TOEIC® L&Rテスト 飛躍のナビゲーター Part 7

濱﨑潤之輔 著

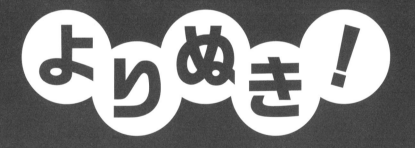

よりぬき！

 OpenGate

音声ファイルの利用方法

　本書では、英文を記憶にストックするための音読トレーニング用素材として、問題文に使用した「文書」と代表的な「設問」例の音声をダウンロードできるようにしました。Chapter 2 および Chapter 4 の音読トレーニングで活用し、英文を自分の中にストックしていきましょう。

1. abceed アプリ（スマートフォンの場合）

本書の音声は、無料アプリ abceed でダウンロードして聴くことができます。

❶ ページ下の QR コードまたは URL から、無料アプリ abceed（Android / iOS 対応）をダウンロードしてください。

❷ 画面下の「見つける（虫めがねのアイコン）」タブをクリックして、本書タイトルで検索します。表示された書影をタップし、音声の項目を選択すると、音声一覧画面へ遷移します。

❸ 再生したいトラックを選択すると音声が再生できます。また、倍速再生、区間リピートなど、学習に便利な機能がついています。

＊アプリの詳細については www.abceed.com にてご確認ください。

〈画面イメージ〉

 ダウンロードはこちらから

https://www.abceed.com
abceed は株式会社 Globee の商品です。

アプリについてのお問い合わせ先
info@globeejp.com
（受付時間：平日の 10 時 -18 時）

2. 弊社ホームページ（PC の場合）

下記 URL より弊社・株式会社オープンゲートのホームページにアクセスしていただき、本書の書影をクリックしてください。

https://openg.jp/

本書の紹介ページを下方にスクロールして

パソコンへのダウンロードはこちら をクリックしてダウンロードしてください。

お問い合わせ先▶株式会社オープンゲート　Tel. 03-5213-4125（受付時間：平日の 10 時 -18 時）

はじめに

　この度、オープンゲートさんから大里秀介さんと共に『TOEIC L&R テスト よりぬきシリーズ』を出版させていただくことになりました。

　Part 7 は読解問題です。
　問題数もリーディングセクション全 100 問のうち 54 問という過半数を占めます。
　英文そのものは決して難解なものが出題されるわけではありませんが、与えられる制限時間に対して圧倒的に解答するのに必要な時間が足りない、という声をよく耳にします。
　実際、900 点〜990 点というハイレベルなスコアを取ることのできる学習者でさえ、「Part 7 を解く時間がもう少し欲しい」という方が非常に多いです。

　余裕を持ってリーディングセクションを解き終えることができるようになるのは、900 点以上のスコアが取れるような実力が伴わなければなかなか簡単ではありません。
　そのレベルに達するためには、何をやればいいのか。
　Part 7 を攻略するための「王道」を明確に提示し、きちんと実力を上げていくには何をすればいいのか。
　どのようなことを知っていればいいのか。
　どんなトレーニングをすればいいのか。
　それらが明瞭に読者のみなさまに伝わるよう工夫して本書を制作しました。

　扱っている英文の種類はそれほど多くはありませんが、出題されるほぼ全てのパターンの英文に対応できるタイプの英文を厳選して掲載し、しっかりと最新の出題傾向に合わせた内容に仕上げています。
　TOEIC L&R テストに出題される英文に正面から向き合い、無駄なく効率よく「読んで解く」ことができるようになるエッセンスをコンパクトに詰め込んだ 1 冊になっています。

本書を使って繰り返し学習し、読解トレーニングを積めば、必ずやあなたの英文読解力は向上し、読解スピードも正答率も飛躍的に上がるはずだと自負しています。

　本書を何回も何回も繰り返してお使いいただくことにより、学ぶたびにあらたな気づきを得ることができるはずです。

　目標までの道のりは決して短くはありませんが、最後まであなたが「学びぬく」ことができますよう、心より応援しています。

　がんばっていきましょう。

2020 年 9 月　濵﨑潤之輔

CONTENTS

Chapter

1

Chapter

2

本書の構成と使い方

本書では、TOEIC® L&R テスト Part 7 の解答スピードと正答率の向上、スコアアップを目指すための「解き方」や、英文を自分の中にストックしていくための「トレーニング」を以下の流れに従って進めます。

■ 本書の構成

Chapter 1

❶ よりぬき！テストの問題を解く！

↓

❷ 解説を読んで解き方のポイントを学ぶ！

最初に、シングルパッセージ15問、ダブルパッセージ5問、トリプルパッセージ5問、合計25問の「よりぬき！テスト」を解き、解説を読み進めながらPart 7の解き方の手順やポイントを確認していきます。

Chapter 2

↓

❶ Part 7 の概要を理解する！

↓

❷ Part 7 の攻略法を知る！

Part 7で出題される典型的な文書や設問のタイプを詳しく見ていきながら、Part 7の概要をつかみ、タイプごとの正解の導き出し方やコツを習得します。
また、リーディングセクション全100問（うちPart 7は54問）を75分で解答するためのタイムマネジメント、および読解スピードを上げるためにするべきことなどを知ります。

↓

❸ 英文の読み方を身に付ける！

英文を英語の語順のまま左から右に一方通行で読むためのトレーニング「スラッシュリーディング」の手法を身に付けます。

↓

❹ トレーニングで英文を ストックする！

「よりぬき！テスト」の文書を使い、スラッシュリーディングの実践をして「英語を見た瞬間に日本語訳を言える」ようにします。さらに、このようにして記憶に蓄えた英文を、お手本になる音声を聴きながらまねをする「音読トレーニング」を行います。これを繰り返すことで、「英語のまま理解できる」英文をどんどんストックしていきます。

❺ トレーニングで設問を ストックする！

また同様のトレーニングで Part 7 の設問を「ひと目で分かる」ようにします。

これらの実践トレーニングによって、Part 7（読解問題）の読解力と読解スピードを上げ、解答スピードの向上とスコアアップの実現を目指します。
なお、この実践トレーニングを今後も続けていけば TOEIC® L&R テストのスコアアップだけでなく、英語の総合力を高めることにつながるはずです。

Chapter 3

❶ 確認テストの問題を 解く！

Chapter 1 の「よりぬき！テスト」と同様、全 25 問の「確認テスト」を解き、解説で解き方のポイントを確認します。

❷ 解説を読んで解き方の ポイントを学ぶ！

Chapter 4

❶ トレーニングで英文の ストックを増やす！

Chapter 2 で実践したときと同様、「確認テスト」の文書を使って、英文ストックを増やすためのトレーニングを行います。

■ 本書の使い方

解説の流れ：問題（文書）→日本語訳→語句→設問→正解→解説→ One-up

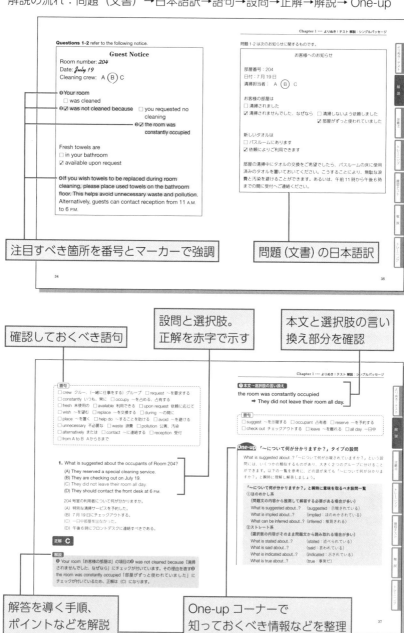

注目すべき箇所を番号とマーカーで強調

問題（文書）の日本語訳

確認しておくべき語句

設問と選択肢。
正解を赤字で示す

本文と選択肢の言い換え部分を確認

解答を導く手順、
ポイントなどを解説

One-up コーナーで
知っておくべき情報などを整理

10

攻略法：Part 7（読解問題）とは何か？を詳しく理解し、解法のポイントやコツ、タイムマネジメント（時間の使い方）などを身に付ける

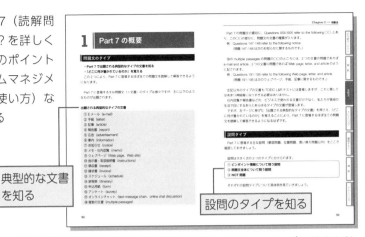

トレーニング：英文を英語の語順のまま、左から右に一方通行で読むトレーニング

英文を／（スラッシュ）で区切り、返り読みをせずに左から右に一方通行で意味をつかむ練習をする

スラッシュリーディングで英語の語順のまま意味をつかめるようになった英文を使い、音読トレーニングを行う。お手本の英語を聴いて、音読する（まねする）

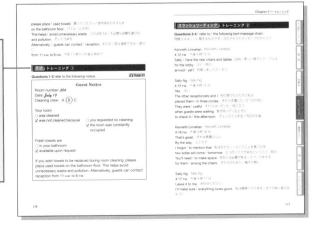

TOEIC® L&R テストについて

TOEIC とは、Test of English for International Communication の略称で、英語を母国語としない人を対象とした、英語によるコミュニケーション能力を測定するテストです。アメリカの非営利機関 ETS (Educational Testing Service) が開発・制作しています。世界各国で実施されており、日本では年間 200 万人以上が受験しています。L&R は Listening and Reading の略で、英語で「聞く」「読む」力を測ります。

◎年 10 回、全国約 80 都市で実施されます
◎テストはすべて英文で構成されています
◎解答方法は全問マークシート方式です
◎合格・不合格ではなく、10〜990 点のスコアで評価されます

L&R テストはリスニングセクションとリーディングセクションの 2 つで構成されており、途中休憩なしの 2 時間で Part 1 から Part 7 まで全 200 問を解答します。

Listening (約 45 分間・100 問)	Part 1	写真描写問題	6 問
	Part 2	応答問題	25 問
	Part 3	会話問題	39 問
	Part 4	説明文問題	30 問
Reading (75 分間・100 問)	Part 5	短文穴埋め問題	30 問
	Part 6	長文穴埋め問題	16 問
	Part 7	読解問題	54 問

申し込み方法等、受験に関する詳細は公式サイトをご覧ください。

● 一般財団法人 国際ビジネスコミュニケーション協会 (IIBC) TOEIC 公式サイト
https://www.iibc-global.org/toeic.html

● 問い合わせ先

IIBC 試験運営センター

〒100-0014

東京都千代田区永田町 2-14-2　山王グランドビル

電話：03-5521-6033　FAX：03-3581-4783

(土・日・祝日・年末年始を除く 10：00〜17：00)

名古屋事務所

電話：052-220-0286

(土・日・祝日・年末年始を除く 10：00〜17：00)

大阪事務所

電話：06-6258-0224

(土・日・祝日・年末年始を除く 10：00〜17：00)

Part 7 基本情報と特徴

テスト形式

読解問題。1つの文書（Single passages・シングルパッセージ）に関する問題が29問、複数の文書（Multiple passages・マルチプルパッセージ）に関する問題が25問。

設問は No. 147〜200まで、合計54問出題されます。

設問を読んで4つの選択肢の中から最も適切なものを選び解答用紙にマークします。

前半の No. 147〜175までは1つの文書（シングルパッセージ）の問題が続き、各文書に設問が2〜4問ずつあります。

後半の複数の文書の問題のうち、No. 176〜185までは2つの文書（Double passages・ダブルパッセージ）の問題が2セット、No. 186〜200までは3つの文書（Triple passages・トリプルパッセージ）の問題が3セットで、1セットにつき設問が5問ずつあります。

＊本書は Part 7 だけを扱いますので、Chapter 1「よりぬき！テスト」、Chapter 3「確認テスト」のいずれも No. は Question 1 から始めています。

Part 7 の特徴

リーディングセクションの Part 7 には、Eメール、手紙、広告のような日常的なものから、請求書や社内回覧のようなビジネス文書、旅程表やアンケートのような表形式のものなど、様々な文書が印刷されています。それらを限られた時間の中で読み、文書全体の理解を問う設問やピンポイント情報について問う設問などに解答します。

具体的な文書タイプや設問パターンは Chapter2 で紹介しますが、通常の問題に加えて、以下のタイプが TOEIC Part 7 の特徴的な問題として出題されます。

① 意図問題：ある発言に関して、発言者がその発言を行った意図を問う問題

→ 2 セット出題されるオンラインチャット（text-message chain、online chat discussion）問題において、各 1 題ずつ出題されます（いずれもシングルパッセージで、計 2 題の出題）。

② 位置問題：文書内に新たな一文を挿入するのに最も適切な箇所を選ぶ問題

→ シングルパッセージの問題 2 セットにおいて、各 1 題ずつ出題されます（計 2 題の出題）。

③ 言い換え問題：問題文中にある語句とほぼ同じ意味の語句を選ぶ問題

→ Part 7 の問題中で、1～3 題ほど出題されます。

Part 7 は出題パターンが多いので、様々な解答アプローチが要求されるパートとなりますが、特に特徴的な上記①～③に関しては、本書で扱う問題の解説で詳しく解答法を扱います。

Chapter

**よりぬき！テスト
問題**

Guest Notice

Room number: *204*

Date: *July 19*

Cleaning crew: A (B) C

Your room

☐ was cleaned

☑ was not cleaned because   ☐ you requested no cleaning

☑ the room was constantly occupied

Fresh towels are

☐ in your bathroom

☑ available upon request

If you wish towels to be replaced during room cleaning, please place used towels on the bathroom floor. This helps avoid unnecessary waste and pollution. Alternatively, guests can contact reception from 11 A.M. to 6 P.M.

1. What is suggested about the occupants of Room 204?

    (A) They reserved a special cleaning service.

    (B) They are checking out on July 19.

    (C) They did not leave their room all day.

    (D) They should contact the front desk at 6 P.M.

2. What is indicated about the hotel?

    (A) It offers multiple cleaning times.

    (B) It has an environmental policy.

    (C) Room cleaning is only done on request.

    (D) There is currently a problem with laundry services.

解説

攻略法

トレーニング

確認テスト

解説

トレーニング

Questions 3-4 refer to the following text-message chain.

Kenneth Linnehan   4:12 P.M.
Sally, have the new chairs and tables for the lobby arrived yet?

Sally Ng   4:15 P.M.
Yes. The other receptionists and I placed them in three circles. They were useful when guests were waiting to check in this afternoon.

Kenneth Linnehan   4:16 P.M.
That's great. By the way, I forgot to mention that two sofas will come tomorrow. You'll need to make space for them among the chairs.

Sally Ng   4:17 P.M.
Leave it to me. I'll make sure everything looks good.

3. In what industry do the people most likely work?

(A) Manufacturing
(B) Hospitality
(C) Health
(D) Design

4. At 4:17 P.M., what does Ms. Ng most likely mean when she writes, "Leave it to me"?

(A) She will cancel a delivery.
(B) She will tell staff members to work late.
(C) She will leave an order sheet on the table.
(D) She will rearrange some furniture.

A Company on the Up

Sci-kid Toys has been getting a lot of media attention lately for its imaginative science toys and kits. But success didn't come immediately for the company.

Founders Ron and Amanda Leyton, a married couple from Inverness, became disappointed when looking for stimulating toys for their 5-year-old son, Lucas. "There was nothing that required thought or skill", said Ron. So, three years ago, they started making toys with Lucas using their own ideas. Amanda explains, "We used household objects and wood to make moving cars, bottle rockets, and model cranes. Lucas loved it!"

Spotting a business opportunity, the pair started selling instructional booklets for their toys. However, the plans were soon copied and shared over the Internet. After a hard six months of little profit, they decided to change focus. Ron says, "We thought of how to monetize our plans. Instead of just the booklets, we offered kits with all the parts needed to make the toys. That was a turning point. Parents liked the convenience of it, and the price was much lower than store-bought toys."

And now, two years after that crucial decision, sales of Sci-kid kits are around $200,000 per month. The company has plans to expand their range and begin overseas sales. And Lucas still loves playing with his original toys!

5. What is the article mainly about?

(A) Methods for teaching young children

(B) Ways to launch an Internet business

(C) A company's change of direction

(D) A couple's search for cheap materials

6. What problem did the Leytons encounter?

(A) There were few opportunities to make money.

(B) They could not afford to recruit staff.

(C) No one was interested in their booklets.

(D) A rival company started selling similar items.

7. When did the kits go on sale?

(A) Two months ago

(B) Six months ago

(C) Two years ago

(D) Three years ago

February 10, Somersanville —Stanley Berg, founder of E-Wave Burger, has been named the Small Business Owner of the Year by the State Chamber of Commerce. — [1] — . Gabe McCrane, vice president of the Chamber, nominated Mr. Berg for the award, basing his decision on the company's steady growth, innovation, and overall contribution to the local community. — [2] — . Those who know him believe that the main reason for the company's success is the founder's enthusiasm and longtime love for the restaurant business.

— [3] — . He cites his mother's management skills as his inspiration for getting involved in the industry. After graduating from Waloo University in Chicago, he opened two restaurants with the financial backing of a local investor. "Both locations were doing well, but after the birth of my fourth child, running these restaurants became overwhelming," Mr. Berg explained. "So, I began thinking about how I could possibly use technology to reduce the need for labor —including my own."

He finally decided to roll out an entirely new line of dining places. — [4] — . Partnering with Hania Ustad, his college classmate and owner of LA Botics Co., he launched the first of several partially automated delis. These delis specialize in simple meals such as hamburgers and sandwiches, items that are relatively simple for robots to create. The food is then carried to the tables by conveyor belts or robots on wheels. Best of all, since the delis have less than 30% of competitors' staffing levels, they are able to save money and pass on the benefits to customers in the form of lower prices.

8. What did Mr. McCrane do?

(A) He selected Mr. Berg for a prize.
(B) He helped establish a firm.
(C) He designed automated systems.
(D) He donated to the community.

9. Why did Mr. Berg change his business?

(A) The firm did not produce enough profit.
(B) His college friend persuaded him quit.
(C) Restaurant operations became difficult.
(D) Technology firms urged him to do so.

10. What is suggested about Ms. Ustad?

(A) She teaches at a university.
(B) She studied in Chicago.
(C) She was raised in Somersanville.
(D) She took courses in food science.

11. In which of the positions marked [1], [2], [3], and [4] does the following sentence best belong?

"Mr. Berg was only twelve when his parents opened their family restaurant and he was instantly impressed by it."

(A) [1]
(B) [2]
(C) [3]
(D) [4]

Questions 12-15 refer to the following online chat discussion.

	⊗ ⊖ ⊕

Gavin Page   (10:13 A.M.)

Hi everyone. I want to inform you about some changes that will soon take place.

Vida Maras   (10:14 A.M.)

I've heard some rumors. What are the specifics?

Gavin Page   (10:16 A.M.)

We're going to be cutting some of our operations staff in Minneapolis and London, but increasing R&D staff in Bangalore and Warsaw.

Abdul Razak   (10:17 A.M.)

What about my department?

Gavin Page   (10:19 A.M.)

Accounting will undergo the biggest changes. We're going to be outsourcing nearly all of those functions. We'll only keep you and a small team in our Boston headquarters.

Abdul Razak   (10:20 A.M.)

Well, I did not see this coming. We posted record profits last year!

Gavin Page   (10:22 A.M.)

I know, but the board thinks we need to cut costs to position us for a stronger performance next year.

Vikram Laghari   (10:24 A.M.)

When will this process start? It's already hard enough to find technical staff here in Bangalore. Now, you seem to be giving me new recruiting targets.

Gavin Page   (10:26 A.M.)

This is all I can tell you at the moment. Management will issue a memo in a few days, and each department head will get detailed instructions before our next big meeting.

12. Why did Mr. Page start the online chat discussion?

(A) To ask for information
(B) To share some news
(C) To confirm some rumors
(D) To provide feedback on a complaint

13. What does Mr. Razak find surprising?

(A) The downsizing of an office branch
(B) The outsourcing of IT tasks at a firm
(C) The election of a new company president
(D) The relocation of a headquarters

14. At 10:22 A.M., what does Mr. Page most likely mean when he writes, "I know"?

(A) He receives regular updates on a policy.
(B) He is aware of the reasons for a change.
(C) He thinks the board is making a mistake.
(D) He acknowledges an achievement.

15. What project will Ms. Laghari be responsible for?

(A) Finding new workplaces for bookkeepers
(B) Hiring technical specialists for the firm
(C) Arranging a presentation for directors
(D) Improving the performance of a department

Questions 16-20 refer to the following Web site and e-mail.

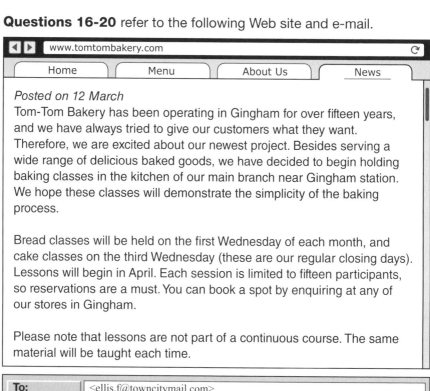

www.tomtombakery.com

| Home | Menu | About Us | News |

Posted on 12 March

Tom-Tom Bakery has been operating in Gingham for over fifteen years, and we have always tried to give our customers what they want. Therefore, we are excited about our newest project. Besides serving a wide range of delicious baked goods, we have decided to begin holding baking classes in the kitchen of our main branch near Gingham station. We hope these classes will demonstrate the simplicity of the baking process.

Bread classes will be held on the first Wednesday of each month, and cake classes on the third Wednesday (these are our regular closing days). Lessons will begin in April. Each session is limited to fifteen participants, so reservations are a must. You can book a spot by enquiring at any of our stores in Gingham.

Please note that lessons are not part of a continuous course. The same material will be taught each time.

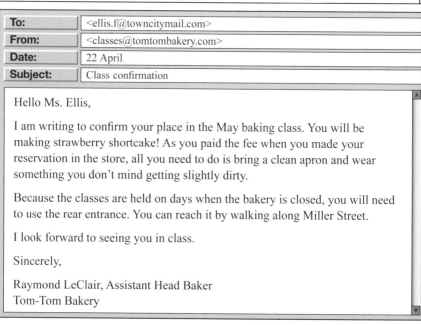

To:	<ellis.f@towncitymail.com>
From:	<classes@tomtombakery.com>
Date:	22 April
Subject:	Class confirmation

Hello Ms. Ellis,

I am writing to confirm your place in the May baking class. You will be making strawberry shortcake! As you paid the fee when you made your reservation in the store, all you need to do is bring a clean apron and wear something you don't mind getting slightly dirty.

Because the classes are held on days when the bakery is closed, you will need to use the rear entrance. You can reach it by walking along Miller Street.

I look forward to seeing you in class.

Sincerely,

Raymond LeClair, Assistant Head Baker
Tom-Tom Bakery

16. Why did the bakery decide to start the classes?

(A) To promote their new products
(B) To highlight how easy baking is
(C) To train part-time staff
(D) To encourage people to open bakeries

17. What is indicated about Tom-Tom Bakery?

(A) It teaches classes in schools.
(B) It closes for one day each week.
(C) It operates multiple outlets in Gingham.
(D) It has a seating area for eating.

18. In the e-mail, the word "reach" in paragraph 2, line 2, is closest in meaning to

(A) arrive at
(B) meet
(C) obtain
(D) stretch

19. On what date will Ms. Ellis' class most likely be held?

(A) April 7
(B) April 21
(C) May 5
(D) May 19

20. What is Ms. Ellis asked to do?

(A) Bring her payment
(B) Confirm her attendance
(C) Purchase some ingredients
(D) Wear suitable clothing

Questions 21-25 refer to the following Web page, letter, and article.

www.dalehill-town.org.uk/recreation/news

Posted 05 May

Notice of Development at Highmoor Park

The Parks and Recreation department of Dalehill's town council has approved the construction of an all-weather rock-climbing facility at Highmoor Park. The proposals were submitted by unpaid community youth leaders wishing to provide more amenities for the young people of Dalehill. It will be built on an unused grassy area bordering Jacob Street.

Construction will begin on July 10, and the climbing wall is expected to be open to the public at the end of September. The final cost has yet to be confirmed but will appear on this Web site in the coming days.

The council hopes to keep the rock-climbing area free of any entry fees, but it reserves the right to introduce charges if running costs are higher than expected.

May 22

Parks and Recreation Dept.
Dalehill Town Council
21-39 High Road
Dalehill DH5 8UI

To whom it may concern:

I am writing regarding the plans for a rock-climbing area in Highmoor Park, which I learned of on the council Web site. While I recognize the need to provide more things to do for the young people of Dalehill, I believe the proposed site should be reconsidered. Far from being an "unused grassy area", that part of the park is very popular with dog walkers like me. The benches there are frequently used for resting and for eating lunch. I know this as my house is directly opposite the area.

I am sure an alternative location can be found before construction begins.

Regards,

Michael Newton

Young Citizens Delighted With New Facility

(October 24)—Highmoor Park was buzzing with excitement yesterday as the mayor formally opened a new rock-climbing area. The outdoor facility consists of a four-meter high and 35-meter long wall with various hand grips to grab onto. On its first day, over one hundred people enjoyed testing their skills. While most were youngsters, there were quite a few adults having a go, too.

Community youth worker Annabel Brines couldn't be happier, saying, "This is a great way to get not only young people, but all citizens to exercise and enjoy the outdoors."

21. What does the Web page mention about the rock-climbing project?

(A) It is funded by community donations.
(B) It was the idea of local volunteers.
(C) The cost of tickets is expected to rise.
(D) It cannot be used on certain days.

22. What is the purpose of the letter?

(A) To criticize a proposal
(B) To request further information
(C) To suggest ideas for activities
(D) To submit a report of citizens' views

23. What is most likely true about Mr. Newton?

(A) He used to work in construction.
(B) He is an experienced rock climber.
(C) He is head of a local club.
(D) He lives on Jacob Street.

24. What problem did the facility encounter?

(A) Bad weather during construction
(B) A delay in opening
(C) A resistance to entrance fees
(D) Overcrowding on the wall

25. In the article, the word "go" in paragraph 1, line 5, is closest in meaning to

(A) attempt
(B) permission
(C) recommendation
(D) journey

よりぬき！テスト　解答一覧

Part 7	正答
1	C
2	B
3	B
4	D
5	C
6	A
7	C
8	A
9	C
10	B
11	C
12	B
13	A
14	D
15	B
16	B
17	C
18	A
19	D
20	D
21	B
22	A
23	D
24	B
25	A

よりぬき！テスト
解説

Guest Notice

Room number: *204*

Date: *July 19*

Cleaning crew: A ⓑ C

❶Your room

☐ was cleaned

❷☑ was not cleaned because   ☐ you requested no
                                              cleaning

                              ❸☑ the room was
                                         constantly occupied

Fresh towels are

☐ in your bathroom

☑ available upon request

❹If you wish towels to be replaced during room
cleaning, please place used towels on the bathroom
floor. This helps avoid unnecessary waste and pollution.
Alternatively, guests can contact reception from 11 A.M.
to 6 P.M.

問題 1-2 は次のお知らせに関するものです。

お客様へのお知らせ

部屋番号：204
日付：7 月 19 日
清掃担当者：　A　(B)　C

お客様の部屋は
□ 清掃されました
☑ 清掃されませんでした、なぜなら　□ 清掃しないよう依頼しました
　　　　　　　　　　　　　　　　　☑ 部屋がずっと使われていました

新しいタオルは
□ バスルームにあります
☑ 依頼によりご利用できます

部屋の清掃中にタオルの交換をご希望でしたら、バスルームの床に使用済みのタオルを置いておいてください。こうすることにより、無駄な浪費と汚染を避けることができます。あるいは、午前 11 時から午後 6 時までの間に受付へご連絡ください。

---

1. What is suggested about the occupants of Room 204?

(A) They reserved a special cleaning service.

(B) They are checking out on July 19.

(C) They did not leave their room all day.

(D) They should contact the front desk at 6 P.M.

204 号室の利用者について何が分かりますか。

(A) 特別な清掃サービスを予約した。

(B) 7 月 19 日にチェックアウトする。

(C) 一日中部屋を出なかった。

(D) 午後 6 時にフロントデスクに連絡すべきである。

正解　C

解説

❶ Your room「お客様の部屋は」の項目の❷ was not cleaned because「清掃されませんでした、なぜなら」にチェックが付いています。その理由を表す❸ the room was constantly occupied「部屋がずっと使われていました」にチェックが付いているため、正解は（C）になります。

❗本文→選択肢の言い換え

the room was constantly occupied
 ➡ They did not leave their room all day.

┌─ 語句 ─────────────────────────────────────┐
│ □ suggest 〜を示唆する　□ occupant 占有者　□ reserve 〜を予約する
│ □ check out チェックアウトする　□ leave 〜を離れる　□ all day 一日中
└──┘

One-up 「〜について何が分かりますか？」タイプの設問

What is suggested about...?「〜について何が示唆されていますか？」という設問には、いくつかの類似するものがあり、大きく2つのグループに分けることができます。以下の一覧を参考に、どの語が来ても「〜について何が分かりますか？」と瞬時に理解し解答しましょう。

「〜について何が分かりますか？」と瞬時に意味を取るべき設問一覧

①ほのめかし系
（問題文の内容から推測して解答する必要がある場合が多い）
What is suggested about...?　（suggested：示唆されている）
What is implied about...?　（implied：ほのめかされている）
What can be inferred about...?　（inferred：推測される）
②ストレート系
（選択肢の内容がそのまま問題文から読み取れる場合が多い）
What is stated about...?　（stated：述べられている）
What is said about...?　（said：言われている）
What is indicated about...?　（indicated：示されている）
What is true about...?　（true：事実だ）

2. What is indicated about the hotel?

(A) It offers multiple cleaning times.
(B) It has an environmental policy.
(C) Room cleaning is only done on request.
(D) There is currently a problem with laundry services.

ホテルについて何が示されていますか。

(A) 清掃を複数回提供している。
(B) 環境方針がある。
(C) 客室清掃は依頼に応じてのみ行われる。
(D) ランドリーサービスに現在問題がある。

正解 B

解説

「ホテルについて何が分かりますか？」と、瞬時に設問の文意を理解します。お知らせの下部に ❹ If you wish towels to be replaced during room cleaning, please place used towels on the bathroom floor. This helps avoid unnecessary waste and pollution. 「部屋の清掃中にタオルの交換をご希望でしたら、バスルームの床に使用済みのタオルを置いておいてください。こうすることにより、無駄な浪費と汚染を避けることができます」とあります。これを端的に述べている (B) が正解です。

❶ 本文→選択肢の言い換え

avoid unnecessary waste and pollution
　　➡ has an environmental policy

┌─**語句**─────────────────────────────────┐
│ □ indicate 〜を示す　□ offer 〜を提供する　□ multiple 複数の
│ □ environmental 環境の　□ policy 方針　□ on request 依頼に応じて
│ □ currently 現在　□ laundry service ランドリーサービス
└──────────────────────────────────────┘

One-up　help ＋動詞の原形

This helps avoid unnecessary waste and pollution. では、helps avoid という「help ＋動詞の原形」が使われています。これは helps to avoid にある to が落ちた形だと考えてください。

Questions 3-4 refer to the following text-message chain.

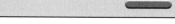

Kenneth Linnehan   4:12 P.M.

Sally, have the new chairs and tables for the lobby arrived yet?

Sally Ng   4:15 P.M.

Yes. ❶The other receptionists and I placed them in three circles. They were useful when guests were waiting to check in this afternoon.

Kenneth Linnehan   4:16 P.M.

That's great. ❷By the way, I forgot to mention that two sofas will come tomorrow. You'll need to make space for them among the chairs.

Sally Ng   4:17 P.M.

❸<u>Leave it to me</u>. I'll make sure everything looks good.

問題 3-4 は次のテキストメッセージのやりとりに関するものです。

Kenneth Linnehan　　　　午後 4 時 12 分
Sally、ロビー用の新しい椅子とテーブルはもう届いていますか。

Sally Ng　　　　午後 4 時 15 分
はい。他の受付係と私とで、それらを 3 つの円形に設置しました。今日の午後お客様がチェックインを待っているときに、それらは役に立ちました。

Kenneth Linnehan　　　　午後 4 時 16 分
それはいいですね。ところで、明日ソファが 2 つ来ることを伝え忘れていました。椅子の間にそれらを置くスペースを作る必要があります。

Sally Ng　　　　午後 4 時 17 分
お任せください。確実に全て見栄えが良くなるようにします。

---

3. In what industry do the people most likely work?

(A) Manufacturing
(B) Hospitality
(C) Health
(D) Design

この人々は何の業界で働いていると考えられますか。

(A) 製造
(B) ホスピタリティ
(C) 医療
(D) デザイン

正解　**B**

解説

Sally さんの午後4時15分の発言に❶ The other receptionists and I placed them in three circles. They were useful when guests were waiting to check in this afternoon. 「他の受付係と私とで、それらを3つの円形に設置しました。今日の午後お客様がチェックインを待っているときに、それらは役に立ちました」とあります。このことから、Kenneth さんと Sally さんは、ホテルのような所で働いているということが推測されます。よって、正解は（B）の Hospitality「ホスピタリティ」です。

🟡 本文→選択肢の言い換え

receptionists, guests, check in ➡ Hospitality

語句

□ industry 業種　□ most likely おそらく

One-up most likely 問題

most likely「おそらく」が設問に含まれている問題は、設問の答えが問題文に明記されておらず、問題文に書かれている内容から「確実に推測できること」が正解になります。問題文にある「具体的」な内容は、選択肢では「抽象的」、「一般的」な表現に言い換えられることが多いのですが、most likely 問題ではそれがより顕著になると考えて取り組むのがベターです。

4. At 4:17 P.M., what does Ms. Ng most likely mean when she writes, "Leave it to me"?

(A) She will cancel a delivery.
(B) She will tell staff members to work late.
(C) She will leave an order sheet on the table.
(D) She will rearrange some furniture.

午後 4 時 17 分に Ng さんが "Leave it to me" と書く際、何を意図していると考えられますか。

(A) 彼女は配送をキャンセルする。
(B) 彼女は従業員に残業するよう伝える。
(C) 彼女は注文書をテーブルの上に置いておく。
(D) 彼女は家具を並べ直す。

正解 D

人物がある発言をした際にどのような意図で述べたかを問う「意図問題」です。
Kenneth さんは午後 4 時 16 分に ❷ By the way, I forgot to mention that two
sofas will come tomorrow. You'll need to make space for them among the
chairs. 「ところで、明日ソファが 2 つ来ることを伝え忘れていました。椅子の
間にそれらを置くスペースを作る必要があります」と述べています。これに対
して Sally さんは ❸ Leave it to me 「お任せください」と伝えていることから、
正解は（D）です。

❗本文→選択肢の言い換え

make space for them (=sofas) among the chairs
　　➡ rearrange some furniture

[語句]

☐ delivery 配達　☐ tell somebody to do 人に〜するように伝える
☐ work late 残業する　☐ leave 〜を置く　☐ order sheet 注文書
☐ rearrange 〜を並べ直す　☐ furniture 家具

One-up　意図問題の解答方法

意図問題はターゲットとなっている発言の前後を読み、その「状況」や「背景」
を理解して、それに合う内容の選択肢を選ぶようにしてください。不正解の選
択肢は多くの場合、前後の文脈に合わないもの、文脈から逸れているものになっ
ていますので、消去法を活用するのも一つの手です。

みんなのお悩み＆おすすめの解答方法 ①

悩み

「英文を読むスピードがまだまだ遅いです。600 点取得が目標なのですが、どの問題であれば解かずに飛ばしてもいいですか？」

解答

　マルチプルパッセージ（ダブルパッセージとトリプルパッセージである 176 番〜200 番までの問題）は、時間に余裕があったら取り組めればいい、という気持ちで臨んでもらえれば十分です。

　時間に万が一余裕ができ、マルチプルパッセージに取り組む場合、ポイントは以下になります。

・各セットの最初の問題だけに挑戦してみましょう

　シングルパッセージの問題と同じく、最初のパッセージを読むだけで解答できる可能性が高いからです。

・単語（や語句）の言い換え問題は全文読まなくても解ける場合が多いです

　言い換え問題は多くの場合、設問にある単語（や語句）の入っている 1 文だけを読めば正解を得られます。

　該当する 1 文だけを読み、設問にある単語（や語句）が「その文中ではどのような意味で使われているのか」を理解し、「その文中での意味」と同じ意味を持つものを選択肢から選びます。

　必ず「文中での意味」を最優先してください。

　設問中にある単語単体と選択肢にある単語単体同士でマッチングさせた場合、不正解になる場合が多々あります。

A Company on the Up

Sci-kid Toys has been getting a lot of media attention lately for its imaginative science toys and kits. But success didn't come immediately for the company.

Founders Ron and Amanda Leyton, a married couple from Inverness, became disappointed when looking for stimulating toys for their 5-year-old son, Lucas. "There was nothing that required thought or skill", said Ron. So, three years ago, they started making toys with Lucas using their own ideas. Amanda explains, "We used household objects and wood to make moving cars, bottle rockets, and model cranes. Lucas loved it!"

Spotting a business opportunity, the pair started selling instructional booklets for their toys. However, the plans were soon copied and shared over the Internet. ❶After a hard six months of little profit, they decided to change focus. Ron says, "We thought of how to monetize our plans. Instead of just the booklets, we offered kits with all the parts needed to make the toys. ❷That was a turning point. Parents liked the convenience of it, and the price was much lower than store-bought toys."

❸And now, two years after that crucial decision, sales of Sci-kid kits are around $200,000 per month. The company has plans to expand their range and begin overseas sales. And Lucas still loves playing with his original toys!

問題 5-7 は次の記事に関するものです。

上昇中の会社

Sci-kid Toys はその独創的な科学玩具やキットで最近メディアの注目をかなり集めてきている。しかしこの会社に成功がすぐに訪れた訳ではない。

　創設者の Ron Leyton と Amanda は Inverness 出身の夫婦で、5 歳の息子 Lucas に良い刺激になるおもちゃを探していたが落胆した。「思考や能力を必要とするものは何もありませんでした」Ron はそう語る。それで 3 年前、彼らは自分たちのアイディアを使って Lucas と一緒におもちゃを作り始めたのだ。Amanda はこう説明する。「私たちは家にある日用品や木材を使って、動く車や瓶のロケット、それにクレーンの模型を作りました。Lucas はとても気に入りました！」

　ビジネスチャンスを見極め、二人は自分たちのおもちゃの教本を販売し始めた。しかし、そのプランはすぐにまねされインターネットで共有されてしまった。ほぼ利益のない苦しい 6 カ月を経て、彼らは目の向けどころを変えようと決意した。Ron はこう話す。「私たちのプランを収益化する方法を考えていました。教本だけというのではなく、おもちゃを作るのに必要な全ての部品を含めたキットを提供したのです。それが転機でした。親御さんたちはその利便性を気に入ってくれ、さらに価格はお店で買うおもちゃよりもずっと低かったです。」

　そして今、重要な決断から 2 年経ち、Sci-kid キットの売り上げは月に約 20 万ドルある。この会社には範囲を拡大し海外への販売を開始する計画がある。そして Lucas は今でもオリジナルのおもちゃで遊ぶのを楽しんでいる！

---

5. What is the article mainly about?

(A) Methods for teaching young children
(B) Ways to launch an Internet business
(C) A company's change of direction
(D) A couple's search for cheap materials

主に何についての記事ですか。

（A）幼児に教える方法
（B）インターネットビジネスを始める方法
（C）ある会社の方向転換
（D）安い材料を求める夫婦の探索

正解 C

解説

問題文全体が、Sci-kid Toys 社が会社の方針を変更し、いかにして成功したかを説明する内容です。第3段落にある❷ That was a turning point.「それが転機でした」や、第4段落にある❸ And now, two years after that crucial decision, sales of Sci-kid kits are around $200,000 per month.「そして今、重要な決断から2年経ち、Sci-kid キットの売り上げは月に約20万ドルある」などに、そのことが端的に表れています。よって、正解は（C）です。

❶ 本文→選択肢の言い換え

a turning point ➡ change of direction

語句
□ mainly 主に　□ method 方法　□ way 方法　□ launch 〜を開始する
□ change of direction 方向転換　□ search 調査、探索　□ material 材料

6. What problem did the Leytons encounter?

(A) There were few opportunities to make money.

(B) They could not afford to recruit staff.

(C) No one was interested in their booklets.

(D) A rival company started selling similar items.

Leyton 夫妻はどのような問題に直面しましたか。

(A) 収益を得る機会がほとんどなかった。

(B) スタッフを採用する余裕がなかった。

(C) 誰も彼らの教本に興味を持たなかった。

(D) 競合他社が同様の商品を販売し始めた。

正解 A

解説

第３段落にある ❶ After a hard six months of little profit, they decided to change focus. 「ほぼ利益のない苦しい６カ月を経て、彼らは目の向けどころを変えようと決意した」とあります。よって、正解は（A）です。

❶ 本文→選択肢の言い換え

a hard six months of little profit

➡ few opportunities to make money

語句

□ encounter ～に直面する　□ few ほとんどない

□ make money お金を稼ぐ　□ afford to do ～する余裕がある

□ recruit （人を）採用する　□ no one 誰も～ない

□ be interested in ～に興味がある　□ rival ライバルの　□ similar 似ている

□ item 商品

7. When did the kits go on sale?

(A) Two months ago
(B) Six months ago
(C) Two years ago
(D) Three years ago

キットはいつ発売されましたか。

(A) 2 カ月前
(B) 6 カ月前
(C) 2 年前
(D) 3 年前

正解 C

解説

第 4 段落にある ❸ And now, two years after that crucial decision, sales of Sci-kid kits are around $200,000 per month.「そして今、重要な決断から 2 年経ち、Sci-kid キットの売り上げは月に約 20 万ドルある」から、重要な決定、すなわち「キットを発売すること」があり、それから 2 年が経ったということがうかがえます。よって、正解は（C）です。

❗本文→選択肢の言い換え

And now, two years after that crucial decision
➡ Two years ago

語句
□ go on sale　発売される

Questions 8-11 refer to the following article.

February 10, Somersanville —Stanley Berg, founder of E-Wave Burger, has been named the Small Business Owner of the Year by the State Chamber of Commerce. — [1] — . ❶Gabe McCrane, vice president of the Chamber, nominated Mr. Berg for the award, basing his decision on the company's steady growth, innovation, and overall contribution to the local community. — [2] — . Those who know him believe that the main reason for the company's success is the founder's enthusiasm and longtime love for the restaurant business.

— [3] — . He cites his mother's management skills as his inspiration for getting involved in the industry. ❷After graduating from Waloo University in Chicago, he opened two restaurants with the financial backing of a local investor. ❸"Both locations were doing well, but after the birth of my fourth child, running these restaurants became overwhelming," Mr. Berg explained. "So, I began thinking about how I could possibly use technology to reduce the need for labor —including my own."

He finally decided to roll out an entirely new line of dining places. — [4] — . ❹Partnering with Hania Ustad, his college classmate and owner of LA Botics Co., ❺he launched the first of several partially automated delis. These delis specialize in simple meals such as hamburgers and sandwiches, items that are relatively simple for robots to create. The food is then carried to the tables by conveyor belts or robots on wheels. Best of all, since the delis have less than 30% of competitors' staffing levels, they are able to save money and pass on the benefits to customers in the form of lower prices.

問題 8-11 は次の記事に関するものです。

2 月 10 日、Somersanville — E-Wave バーガーの創設者、Stanley Berg は州商工会議所により年間の最優秀中小企業経営者に指名された。— [1] — 商工会議所副会頭の Gabe McCrane が Berg 氏をこの賞に推薦したが、彼の決定は会社の着実な成長、改革、そして地域社会への総合的な貢献に基づいている。— [2] — 彼を知る人は、会社の成功の主な要因は創設者の熱意とレストランビジネスへの長年の愛情だと信じている。

— [3] — 彼はこの業界へ関わる着想として自身の母親の経営能力を引き合いに出している。Chicago にある Waloo 大学を卒業後、彼は地元の投資者の財政的な後ろ盾の元で 2 軒のレストランをオープンした。「2 つの店舗とも順調でしたが、4 番目の子供が生まれた後、これらのレストランの経営に圧倒されるようになってきたのです」と Berg 氏は説明した。「それで、労働力の必要性を削減するのにどうやったらテクノロジーを使えるか考え始めました — 自身の労働力も含めて。」

ついに彼は全く新しいタイプのレストランを本格展開する決断をしたのだ。— [4] — 大学のクラスメートであり LA Botics 社のオーナーでもある Hania Ustad と組み、彼は部分的に自動化がなされたいくつかのデリの、最初の店舗を開店した。こうしたデリは、シンプルな食事、例えばハンバーガーやサンドウィッチなどロボットでも作れる比較的シンプルな品に特化している。食べ物はそれからベルトコンベヤーや車輪の付いたロボットによりテーブルへ運ばれる。とりわけ、このデリの人員レベルは競合他社の 30％以下なので、資金を節約してその利益を低価格という形で顧客に還元できるのである。

□ founder 創設者　□ name 〜の名前を挙げる

□ Chamber of Commerce 商工会議所　□ vice president 副会長

□ nominate 〜を推薦する　□ award 賞

□ base A on B AをBに基づかせる　□ decision 決定　□ steady 着実な

□ growth 成長　□ innovation 革新　□ overall 全体的な

□ contribution to 〜への貢献　□ local 地元の　□ community 地域社会

□ those who 〜する人たち　□ enthusiasm 熱意　□ cite 〜を引用する

□ management 経営、管理　□ skill 技能　□ as 〜として

□ inspiration for 〜への着想　□ get involved in 〜に関わる

□ industry 業界　□ after doing 〜した後で　□ graduate from 〜を卒業する

□ financial 財政的な　□ backing 後ろ盾　□ investor 投資家

□ location 店舗　□ run 〜を経営する　□ overwhelming 圧倒する

□ explain 説明する　□ begin doing 〜し始める

□ could possibly do ひょっとして〜できるかもしれない

□ reduce 〜を減らす　□ labor 労働力　□ including 〜を含めて

□ finally ついに　□ decide to do 〜することに決める

□ roll out 〜を本格展開する　□ entirely 完全に

□ new line of 新しい種類の〜　□ partner with 〜と提携する

□ launch 〜を開始する　□ partially 部分的に　□ automated 自動化された

□ deli（総菜などの）販売コーナー、デリ（カテッセン）

□ specialize in 〜を専門とする　□ such as 〜のような　□ item 商品

□ relatively 比較的　□ create 〜を作る　□ be carried to 〜へ運ばれる

□ on wheels 車輪付きの　□ best of all 特に　□ since 〜なので

□ competitor 競合他社　□ staffing level 職員のレベル

□ be able to do 〜することができる　□ pass on 〜を渡す　□ benefit 恩恵

□ in the form of 〜という形で

8. What did Mr. McCrane do?

(A) He selected Mr. Berg for a prize.
(B) He helped establish a firm.
(C) He designed automated systems.
(D) He donated to the community.

McCrane 氏は何をしましたか。

(A) 彼は Berg 氏を受賞者に選出した。
(B) 彼は会社を設立する手助けをした。
(C) 彼は自動化システムを設計した。
(D) 彼は地域社会に寄付をした。

正解 A

解説

第 1 段 落 に ❶ Gabe McCrane, vice president of the Chamber, nominated Mr. Berg for the award, basing his decision on the company's steady growth, innovation, and overall contribution to the local community.「商工会議所副会頭の Gabe McCrane が Berg 氏をこの賞に推薦したが、彼の決定は会社の着実な成長、改革、そして地域社会への総合的な貢献に基づいている」とあります。問題文にある nominated「〜を推薦した」が選択肢では selected「〜を選んだ」に、award「賞」が選択肢では prize「賞」にそれぞれ言い換えられています。正解は (A) です。

❶本文→選択肢の言い換え

nominated Mr. Berg for the award
➡ selected Mr. Berg for a prize

語句

□ select 〜を選ぶ　□ prize 賞　□ help do 〜　するのを助ける
□ establish 〜を設立する　□ firm 会社　□ design 〜を設計する
□ donate to 〜に寄付をする

9. Why did Mr. Berg change his business?

(A) The firm did not produce enough profit.
(B) His college friend persuaded him to quit.
(C) Restaurant operations became difficult.
(D) Technology firms urged him to do so.

Berg 氏はなぜ自身の事業を変えたのですか。

(A) 会社は十分な利益を生み出していなかった。
(B) 彼の大学の友人が彼にやめるよう説得した。
(C) レストランの運営が困難になった。
(D) テクノロジー企業が彼にそうするよう勧めた。

正解 C

解説

第 2 段落に ❸ "Both locations were doing well, but after the birth of my fourth child, running these restaurants became overwhelming," 「2 つの店舗とも順調でしたが、4 番目の子供が生まれた後、これらのレストランの経営に圧倒されるようになってきたのです」とあります。この後、第 3 段落に ❺ he launched the first of several partially automated delis 「彼は部分的に自動化がなされたいくつかのデリの、最初の店舗を開店した」とあります。レストラン経営が煩雑になり、自動化を取り入れたデリの経営に移行したことが分かるため、正解は (C) です。問題文にある overwhelming 「圧倒する」が、選択肢では difficult 「難しい」に言い換えられています。

❶ 本文→選択肢の言い換え

running these restaurants became overwhelming
➡ Restaurant operations became difficult.

語句

□ produce 〜を生む　□ profit 収益　□ persuade 〜を説得する
□ quit やめる　□ operation 運営
□ urge somebody to do 人に〜するように促す

Chapter 1 >>> よりぬき！テスト 解説：シングルパッセージ

One-up overwhelming の使い方

overwhelming は「圧倒的な、圧倒する」という意味の形容詞ですが、become overwhelming で「（主語に）圧迫されそうになる」という意味になります。

10. What is suggested about Ms. Ustad?

(A) She teaches at a university.
(B) She studied in Chicago.
(C) She was raised in Somersanville.
(D) She took courses in food science.

Ustad さんについて何が分かりますか。

(A) 彼女は大学で教えている。
(B) 彼女は Chicago で学んだ。
(C) 彼女は Somersanville で育った。
(D) 彼女は食品科学のコースを取った。

正解 B

解説

第 3 段落に❹ Partnering with Hania Ustad, his college classmate and owner of LA Botics Co.「彼（Berg 氏）の大学のクラスメートであり LA Botics 社のオーナーでもある Hania Ustad と組み」とあります。また、第 2 段落に❷ After graduating from Waloo University in Chicago「（Berg 氏が）Chicago にある Waloo 大学を卒業した後」とあることから、Ustad さんは Chicago にある Waloo 大学に通っていたことが分かります。よって、正解は（B）です。

❶本文→選択肢の言い換え

graduating from Waloo University in Chicago
➡ studied in Chicago

語句
☐ be raised in ～で育つ ☐ course 課程、コース ☐ food science 食品科学

57

After graduating「〜を卒業した後」は、元は After he graduated ですが、主語が省略され、接続詞の後ろに直接動詞の ing 形が続いた形です。主語の省略などによって接続詞や前置詞の後ろに ing 形が続く頻出のものをまとめておきます。

before doing	「〜する前に」
after doing	「〜した後で」
when doing	「〜するときに」
while doing	「〜している間に」
since doing	「〜して以来」
by doing	「〜することによって」

11. In which of the positions marked [1], [2], [3], and [4] does the following sentence best belong?

"Mr. Berg was only twelve when his parents opened their family restaurant and he was instantly impressed by it."

(A) [1]

(B) [2]

(C) [3]

(D) [4]

[1]、[2]、[3] および [4] と記載された箇所のうち、次の文が入るのに最もふさわしいのはどれですか。

「Berg 氏の両親がファミリーレストランをオープンした時、彼はまだ 12 歳だったが、すぐに強い印象を受けた。」

(A) [1]

(B) [2]

(C) [3]

(D) [4]

正解 **C**

解説

文を問題文中の正しい位置に置く、位置問題です。挿入する文には Berg 氏の子供の頃のことが書かれているため、挿入すべき位置の前後にはこれに関連する話題があるはずです。Berg 氏の若かりし頃のことについて述べられているのは第 2 段落で、[3] の位置に挿入文を入れると、Berg 氏が 12 歳の頃に両親がレストランを開店した話の次に、母親の経営能力の話や、彼が大学を卒業した後の話へと続き、時系列的にも正しくなります。よって、正解は（C）です。

語句

□ instantly すぐに　□ impressed by ～に深く印象付けられる

One-up 位置問題の解答法

位置問題はそのセットの最後の問題である場合が多いのですが、そうではない場合でも、全文を読み終えた後に解答するようにすると解きやすくなります。前後の文脈から正解となりそうな位置を選び、挿入する文が前後の文の話題に沿っているかどうか、接続詞や副詞、代名詞などが正しく前後にある文や語句に対応しているかを確認し、正解だと思える位置を最終決定するようにします。

Questions 12-15 refer to the following online chat discussion.

❌ ⊖ ⊕

Gavin Page	(10:13 A.M.)

Hi everyone. ❶I want to inform you about some changes that will soon take place.

Vida Maras	(10:14 A.M.)

I've heard some rumors. What are the specifics?

Gavin Page	(10:16 A.M.)

We're going to be cutting some of our operations staff in Minneapolis and London, but increasing R&D staff in Bangalore and Warsaw.

Abdul Razak	(10:17 A.M.)

❷What about my department?

Gavin Page	(10:19 A.M.)

❸Accounting will undergo the biggest changes. We're going to be outsourcing nearly all of those functions. We'll only keep you and a small team in our Boston headquarters.

Abdul Razak	(10:20 A.M.)

❹Well, I did not see this coming. We posted record profits last year!

Gavin Page	(10:22 A.M.)

I know, but the board thinks we need to cut costs to position us for a stronger performance next year.

Vikram Laghari	(10:24 A.M.)

When will this process start? ❺It's already hard enough to find technical staff here in Bangalore. Now, you seem to be giving me new recruiting targets.

Gavin Page	(10:26 A.M.)

This is all I can tell you at the moment. Management will issue a memo in a few days, and each department head will get detailed instructions before our next big meeting.

問題 12-15 は次のオンラインチャットの話し合いに関するものです。

Gavin Page　　　　（午前 10 時 13 分）
みなさんこんにちは。間もなく実行されるいくつかの変更点についてお知らせ
したいのですが。

Vida Maras　　　　（午前 10 時 14 分）
うわさを聞いています。具体的にはどんなことですか。

Gavin Page　　　　（午前 10 時 16 分）
当社は Minneapolis と London の運営スタッフを数名削減するのですが、
Bangalore と Warsaw の研究開発スタッフは増やします。

Abdul Razak　　　　（午前 10 時 17 分）
私の部署はどうなりますか。

Gavin Page　　　　（午前 10 時 19 分）
経理は最も大きく変化します。その機能のほぼ全てを外注する予定です。
Boston 本社に、あなたと少人数のチームだけ残します。

Abdul Razak　　　　（午前 10 時 20 分）
うーん、こうなることは予想していませんでした。私たちは昨年記録的な利益
を上げたのに！

Gavin Page　　　　（午前 10 時 22 分）
そうですよね、でも役員会は来年さらに業績が高まるよう費用を削減して私た
ちを配置する必要があると考えているのです。

Vikram Laghari　　（午前 10 時 24 分）
その工程はいつ始まりますか。ここ Bangalore で技術スタッフを見つけること
は、すでに困難な状況です。では新しい採用目標を与えられるのでしょうね。

Gavin Page　　　　（午前 10 時 26 分）
今のところ伝えられるのはこれだけです。経営陣が数日後に連絡文書を出して、
次の大きな会議までに各部の部長が詳細な指示を受けるでしょう。

よりぬき！テスト

解説

攻略法

トレーニング

確認テスト

解説

トレーニング

> **語句**
>
> ☐ inform 〜に知らせる　☐ take place 行われる　☐ rumor うわさ
> ☐ specific 詳細　☐ operation 運営　☐ increase 〜を増やす
> ☐ R&D 研究開発（research and development）　☐ department 部署
> ☐ accounting 経理　☐ undergo 〜を経験する　☐ outsource 〜を外注する
> ☐ nearly ほとんど　☐ function 機能　☐ headquarters 本社
> ☐ post 〜を打ち立てる　☐ record 記録的な　☐ profit 利益
> ☐ board 役員会　☐ position 〜を適切な場所に置く　☐ performance 業績
> ☐ process （一連の）行為　☐ seem to do 〜するようだ
> ☐ recruit 〜を採用する　☐ at the moment 現在、今のところ
> ☐ management 経営陣　☐ issue 〜を発行する　☐ memo 連絡文書
> ☐ detailed 詳細な　☐ instruction 指示

12. Why did Mr. Page start the online chat discussion?

(A) To ask for information
(B) To share some news
(C) To confirm some rumors
(D) To provide feedback on a complaint

Page 氏がオンラインチャットの話し合いを始めたのはなぜですか。

(A) 情報を求めるため
(B) お知らせを共有するため
(C) うわさを確かめるため
(D) 苦情に関する意見を述べるため

正解 B

【解説】

Page さんは午前 10 時 13 分の発言で、❶ I want to inform you about some changes that will soon take place. 「私は間もなく実行されるいくつかの変更点についてお知らせしたい」と述べています。問題文にある inform you about「〜について知らせる」を share「〜を共有する」に、some changes「いくつかの変更点」を some news「お知らせ」に言い換えている、(B) が正解です。

【❶本文→選択肢の言い換え】

inform you about some changes ➡ share some news

┌─【語句】────────────────────────────────────
│ □ ask for 〜を求める　□ share 〜を共有する　□ confirm 〜を確認する
│ □ provide 〜を提供する　□ feedback 反応、意見　□ complaint 苦情
└───

One-up inform の使い方

inform「〜に知らせる」は、inform somebody of something「人に物を知らせる」、inform somebody that S+V「人に that 以下のことを知らせる」という使い方をします。

13. What does Mr. Razak find surprising?

(A) The downsizing of an office branch
(B) The outsourcing of IT tasks at a firm
(C) The election of a new company president
(D) The relocation of a headquarters

Razak 氏は何が驚くべきことだと思っていますか。

(A) 支店の人員削減
(B) 会社の IT 業務の外部委託
(C) 新社長の選出
(D) 本社の移転

正解 A

解説

午前 10 時 17 分の Razak さんの❷ What about my department?「私の部署はどうなりますか」という発言に対して、午前 10 時 19 分に Page さんは❸ Accounting will undergo the biggest changes. We're going to be outsourcing nearly all of those functions. We'll only keep you and a small team in our Boston headquarters.「経理は最も大きく変化します。その機能のほぼ全てを外注する予定です。Boston 本社に、あなたと少人数のチームだけ残します」と返答しています。これに対して Razak さんは午前 10 時 20 分に❹ Well, I did not see this coming. We posted record profits last year!「うーん、こうなることは予想していませんでした。私たちは昨年記録的な利益を上げたのに」と述べています。Razak さんは、まさか自分の部署がリストラされて縮小されるとは思ってもいなかったということが分かるため、正解は (A) です。

❶本文→選択肢の言い換え

We'll only keep you and a small team in our Boston headquarters. ➡ The downsizing of an office branch

64

語句

☐ find A B　A が B だと分かる　☐ surprising　予期しない、驚くべき
☐ downsizing　人数削減　☐ branch　支店　☐ outsourcing　外注
☐ task　作業、仕事　☐ firm　会社　☐ election　選挙、選出
☐ company president　社長　☐ relocation　移転

One-up 知覚動詞＋目的語＋動詞の原形 or 動詞の ing 形

I did not see this coming.「私はこうなることは予想していませんでした」は、動詞（see）＋目的語（this）＋動詞の ing 形（coming）から成る表現です。知覚動詞＋目的語の後ろには、目的語の行っている動作を動詞の原形や ing 形で置くことができます。
I saw Mr. Takagi enter into the gym.「私は Takagi さんがジムに入るのを見た」
I saw Mr. Takagi entering into the gym.「私は Takagi さんがジムに入っていくのを見た」

---

14. At 10:22 A.M., what does Mr. Page most likely mean when he writes, "I know"?

(A) He receives regular updates on a policy.
(B) He is aware of the reasons for a change.
(C) He thinks the board is making a mistake.
(D) He acknowledges an achievement.

午前 10 時 22 分に Page 氏が "I know" と書く際、何を意図していると考えられますか。
(A) 彼は方針について定期的な最新情報を受けている。
(B) 彼は変更の理由を知っている。
(C) 彼は役員会が間違いをしていると考えている。
(D) 彼は功績を認めている。

正解 D

人物がある発言をする際に、それをどのような意図で述べたかを問う「意図問題」です。Razak さんは午前 10 時 20 分に❹ Well, I did not see this coming. We posted record profits last year!「うーん、こうなることは予想していませんでした。私たちは昨年記録的な利益を上げたのに」と述べています。これに対して Page さんは I know「分かっています」と応答しています。Page さんの言う「分かっています」とは、会社が昨年記録的な利益を上げたことなので、正解は (D) です。

❗本文→選択肢の言い換え

posted record profits last year ➡ an achievement

語句
□ regular 定期的な　□ update 更新情報　□ policy 方針
□ be aware of 〜に気付いている　□ acknowledge 〜を認める
□ achievement 功績

15. What project will Ms. Laghari be responsible for?

(A) Finding new workplaces for bookkeepers
(B) Hiring technical specialists for the firm
(C) Arranging a presentation for directors
(D) Improving the performance of a department

Laghari さんは何のプロジェクトを担当しますか。

(A) 簿記係用の新しい職場を見つけること
(B) 会社の技術専門家を雇うこと
(C) 部長たちに向けたプレゼンテーションを準備すること
(D) 部署の業績を向上させること

正解 **B**

解説

Laghari さんは午前 10 時 24 分の発言で❺ It's already hard enough to find technical staff here in Bangalore. Now, you seem to be giving me new recruiting targets. 「ここ Bangalore で技術スタッフを見つけることは、すでに困難な状況です。では新しい採用目標を与えられるのでしょうね」と述べており、Laghari さんが採用を担当することが分かります。find technical staff 「技術スタッフを見つける」を Hiring technical specialists 「技術専門家を雇うこと」と言い換えて表している (B) が正解です。

❶本文→選択肢の言い換え

find technical staff ➡ Hiring technical specialists

語句

□ be responsible for ～を担当している　□ workplace 職場
□ bookkeeper 簿記係　□ hire ～を雇う　□ technical specialist 技術専門家
□ arrange ～を手配する　□ director 部長　□ improve ～を向上させる

Questions 16-20 refer to the following Web site and e-mail.

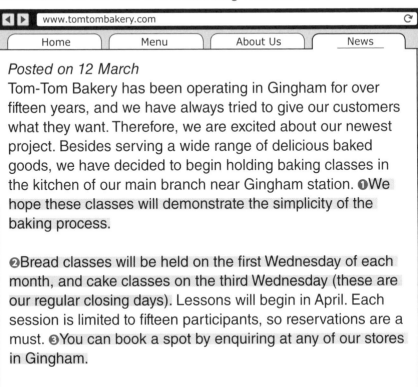

www.tomtombakery.com

| Home | Menu | About Us | News |

Posted on 12 March
Tom-Tom Bakery has been operating in Gingham for over fifteen years, and we have always tried to give our customers what they want. Therefore, we are excited about our newest project. Besides serving a wide range of delicious baked goods, we have decided to begin holding baking classes in the kitchen of our main branch near Gingham station. ❶We hope these classes will demonstrate the simplicity of the baking process.

❷Bread classes will be held on the first Wednesday of each month, and cake classes on the third Wednesday (these are our regular closing days). Lessons will begin in April. Each session is limited to fifteen participants, so reservations are a must. ❸You can book a spot by enquiring at any of our stores in Gingham.

Please note that lessons are not part of a continuous course. The same material will be taught each time.

問題 16-20 は次のウェブサイトと E メールに関するものです。

よりぬき！テスト
解説
攻略法
トレーニング
確認テスト
解説
トレーニング

www.tomtombakery.com
ホーム ｜ メニュー ｜ 当店について ｜ ニュース

3 月 12 日掲載
Tom-Tom Bakery は 15 年以上にわたり Gingham で営業を続け、常にお客様が望むものを提供できるよう努めてきました。そのため、当店の最新のプロジェクトをとても楽しみにしています。様々な美味しい焼き菓子やパンの提供に加え、Gingham 駅の近くにある本店のキッチンにてベーキング教室の開催を始めることに決めました。この教室でベーキングの工程の簡単さを実演できたらと思っています。

パン教室は毎月第 1 水曜日に開催され、ケーキ教室は第 3 水曜日に開催されます（これらは当店の定休日です）。教室は 4 月に始まります。各回とも参加者は 15 名に限られますので、予約が必須です。Gingham のどの店舗でも、お問い合わせいただき、席を予約することができます。

教室は連続したコースの一部ではありませんのでご留意ください。毎回同じ内容が取り扱われます。

語句
□ post 〜を掲載する　□ bakery パン屋　□ operate 〜を経営する
□ try to do 〜しようとする　□ customer 顧客　□ therefore したがって
□ be excited about 〜にわくわくする　□ besides 〜以外に
□ serve （食べ物など）を出す　□ a wide range of 様々な〜
□ delicious 美味しい　□ baked goods 焼き菓子、パン
□ decide to do 〜することに決める　□ hold 〜を開催する
□ baking （パン、ケーキ、クッキーなどを）焼くこと
□ main branch 主たる支店　□ demonstrate 〜を実演する
□ simplicity 簡単さ　□ process 過程　□ be held 行われる
□ each それぞれの　□ regular closing day 定休日
□ be limited to 〜に制限される　□ participant 参加者　□ reservation 予約
□ must 必須　□ book 〜を予約する　□ spot 場所
□ by doing 〜することによって　□ enquire 尋ねる
□ please note that 〜ということにご注意ください
□ continuous 続きものの　□ material 題材

To:	<ellis.f@towncitymail.com>
From:	<classes@tomtombakery.com>
Date:	22 April
Subject:	Class confirmation

Hello Ms. Ellis,

❹I am writing to confirm your place in the May baking class. ❺You will be making strawberry shortcake! As you paid the fee when you made your reservation in the store, ❻all you need to do is bring a clean apron and wear something you don't mind getting slightly dirty.

Because the classes are held on days when the bakery is closed, you will need to use the rear entrance. ❼You can <u>reach</u> it by walking along Miller Street.

I look forward to seeing you in class.

Sincerely,

Raymond LeClair, Assistant Head Baker
Tom-Tom Bakery

宛先：<ellis.f@towncitymail.com>
送信者：<classes@tomtombakery.com>
日付：4月22日
件名：教室の確認

Ellis 様、こんにちは。

5月のベーキング教室についてお客様の席の確認のためご連絡しています。いちごのショートケーキを作ります！ 店頭での予約の際に費用をお支払いいただいていますので、必要なことは清潔なエプロンをお持ちいただき、少し汚れても気にならない衣服を着用することだけです。

教室はベーカリーが休みの日に開催されますので、裏口をご利用いただく必要があります。Miller Street 沿いを歩けばたどり着くことができます。

教室でお会いできるのを楽しみにしています。

よろしくお願いいたします。

Tom-Tom Bakery
パン製造長補佐　Raymond LeClair

語句

□ subject 件名　□ confirmation 確認　□ confirm ～を確認する
□ place 席　□ as ～なので　□ fee 料金
□ make a reservation 予約をする
□ all you need to do is あなたは～しさえすればいい　□ clean 清潔な
□ apron エプロン　□ wear ～を着用する
□ mind doing ～することを気にする　□ slightly 少し　□ dirty 汚い
□ rear entrance 裏口　□ reach ～に着く　□ along ～に沿って
□ look forward to doing ～することを楽しみに待つ
□ sincerely よろしくお願いします

16. Why did the bakery decide to start the classes?

(A) To promote their new products
(B) To highlight how easy baking is
(C) To train part-time staff
(D) To encourage people to open bakeries

ベーカリーが教室を始めると決めたのはなぜですか。

(A) 新商品を宣伝するため
(B) ベーキングがいかに簡単かを強調するため
(C) アルバイトの店員を訓練するため
(D) ベーカリーを開店するよう人々に勧めるため

正解 B

解説

1つ目の文書の第1段落の❶に We hope these classes will demonstrate the simplicity of the baking process. 「この教室でベーキングの工程の簡単さを実演できたらと思っています」とあります。これを端的に言い換えている (B) が正解です。

❶ 本文→選択肢の言い換え

demonstrate the simplicity of the baking process
  ➡ highlight how easy baking is

語句

□ promote ～を宣伝する　□ product 製品　□ highlight ～を強調する
□ train ～を訓練する　□ part-time パートタイムの
□ encourage somebody to do　人が～するのを勧める

One-up decide to do と decide against doing

decide to do は「～することを決める」、decide against doing は「～しないことに決める」という意味になります。

17. What is indicated about Tom-Tom Bakery?

(A) It teaches classes in schools.

(B) It closes for one day each week.

(C) It operates multiple outlets in Gingham.

(D) It has a seating area for eating.

Tom-Tom Bakery について何が示されていますか。

(A) 学校で授業をする。

(B) 毎週1日閉店する。

(C) Gingham で複数の店舗を運営する。

(D) 食事をするための座席エリアがある。

正解 C

解説

1つ目の文書の第2段落❸に You can book a spot by enquiring at any of our stores in Gingham.「Gingham のどの店舗でも、お問い合わせいただき、席を予約することができます」とあります。any of our stores in Gingham から、Gingham に店舗が複数あることが分かるので、正解は（C）です。

❶本文→選択肢の言い換え

any of our stores in Gingham

➡ operates multiple outlets in Gingham

語句

□ indicate ～を示す　□ multiple 複数の　□ outlet 販路、販売店

□ seating area 座席区域

よりぬき！テスト

解説

攻略法

トレーニング

確認テスト

解説

トレーニング

18. In the e-mail, the word "reach" in paragraph 2, line 2, is closest in meaning to

(A) arrive at
(B) meet
(C) obtain
(D) stretch

Eメールの第2段落・2行目にある "reach" に最も意味が近いのは

(A) ～に到着する
(B) ～に会う
(C) ～を獲得する
(D) ～を伸ばす

正解　A

解説

2つ目の文書（Eメール）の第2段落❼に You can reach it by walking along Miller Street. 「Miller Street 沿いを歩けばたどり着くことができます」とあります。ここでの reach は「（目的地に）達する」という意味で使われています。これは arrive at 「～に到着する」とほぼ同じ意味で使われているため、正解は (A) です。

語句

□ paragraph 段落　□ be closest in meaning to ～に意味が最も近い

One-up　「～に到着する」を表す表現

① arrive at/in
② reach
③ get to

よりぬき！テスト

19. On what date will Ms. Ellis' class most likely be held?

(A) April 7
(B) April 21
(C) May 5
(D) May 19

Ellis さんのクラスは何日に開催されると考えられますか。

(A) 4月7日
(B) 4月21日
(C) 5月5日
(D) 5月19日

解説

正解 D

解説

1つ目の文書の第2段落❷に Bread classes will be held on the first Wednesday of each month, and cake classes on the third Wednesday (these are our regular closing days).「パン教室は毎月第1水曜日に開催され、ケーキ教室は第3水曜日に開催されます（これらは当店の定休日です）」とあります。また、2つ目の文書（Ellis さん宛のEメール）の第1段落❹に I am writing to confirm your place in the May baking class.「5月のベーキング教室についてお客様の席の確認のためご連絡しています」、❺に You will be making strawberry shortcake!「いちごのショートケーキを作ります！」とあります。上記から、Ellis さんの参加するクラスは5月の第3水曜日に開催されることが分かるため、これに該当しそうなものは (D) の May 19「5月19日」です。

●文書間の言い換え

cake classes ➡ making strawberry shortcake

攻略法

トレーニング

確認テスト

解説

トレーニング

「開催される」を表す表現

① be held
② take place

20. What is Ms. Ellis asked to do?

(A) Bring her payment
(B) Confirm her attendance
(C) Purchase some ingredients
(D) Wear suitable clothing

Ellis さんは何をするよう依頼されていますか。

(A) 支払金を持参する
(B) 出席を確認する
(C) いくらか材料を購入する
(D) 適切な衣服を着用する

正解 **D**

解説

2つ目の文書（Ellis さん宛のEメール）の第1段落の❻に、all you need to do is bring a clean apron and wear something you don't mind getting slightly dirty「必要なことは清潔なエプロンをお持ちいただき、少し汚れても気にならない衣服を着用することだけです」とあります。これを簡潔に言い表している、(D) が正解です。

❶本文→選択肢の言い換え

wear something you don't mind getting slightly dirty
➡ Wear suitable clothing

┌─[語句]───┐
│ □ ask somebody to do 人に〜するように頼む　□ payment 支払金 │
│ □ attendance 出席　□ purchase 〜を購入する　□ ingredient 材料 │
│ □ suitable ふさわしい　□ clothing 衣類 │
└───┘

Questions 21-25 refer to the following Web page, letter, and article.

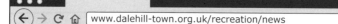

www.dalehill-town.org.uk/recreation/news

Posted 05 May

Notice of Development at Highmoor Park

The Parks and Recreation department of Dalehill's town council has approved the construction of an all-weather rock-climbing facility at Highmoor Park. ❶The proposals were submitted by unpaid community youth leaders wishing to provide more amenities for the young people of Dalehill. ❷It will be built on an unused grassy area bordering Jacob Street.

Construction will begin on July 10, and ❸the climbing wall is expected to be open to the public at the end of September. The final cost has yet to be confirmed but will appear on this Web site in the coming days.

The council hopes to keep the rock-climbing area free of any entry fees, but it reserves the right to introduce charges if running costs are higher than expected.

問題 21-25 は次のウェブページ、手紙、記事に関するものです。

---

www.dalehill-town.org.uk/recreation/news

5月5日掲載

Highmoor 公園の開発に関するお知らせ

Dalehill 町議会の公園緑地部は、Highmoor 公園での全天候型ロッククライミング施設の建設を承認しました。この提案は、より多くの公共施設を Dalehill の若者のために提供してほしいと望んだ、無給の地域の若いリーダーたちによって提出されました。それは Jacob Street に隣接する、利用されていない草地に建てられる予定です。

建設は 7 月 10 日に始まり、このクライミング用の壁は 9 月末に一般に向けてオープンする予定です。最終的な費用はまだ確認されていませんが、近日中にこのウェブサイト上で公表されます。

議会は、このロッククライミングエリアを入場無料にし続けることを望んでいますが、運営費用が予想を上回る場合には有料化する権利を保有しています。

【語句】

☐ development 開発　☐ town council 町議会　☐ approve ～を承認する
☐ construction 建設　☐ all-weather 全天候型の
☐ rock-climbing ロッククライミング　☐ facility 施設　☐ proposal 提案
☐ submit ～を提出する　☐ unpaid 無給の　☐ community 地域
☐ youth 若者　☐ wish to do ～することを望む　☐ provide ～を提供する
☐ amenity アメニティ、公共施設　☐ unused 使われていない
☐ grassy area 草地　☐ border ～に隣接する
☐ climbing wall クライミング用の壁、クライミング・ウォール
☐ be expected to do ～することになっている　☐ be open to ～に開かれる
☐ public 市民　☐ at the end of ～の終わりに　☐ final 最終的な
☐ cost 費用　☐ have yet to do まだ～していない　☐ confirm ～を確認する
☐ appear 現れる　☐ in the coming days 近日中に
☐ hope to do ～することを願う　☐ keep A B A を B のままにする
☐ free 無料の　☐ entry fee 入場料　☐ reserve ～を保持する　☐ right 権利
☐ introduce ～を導入する　☐ charge 料金　☐ running cost 運営費

May 22

Parks and Recreation Dept.
Dalehill Town Council
21-39 High Road
Dalehill DH5 8UI

To whom it may concern:

I am writing regarding the plans for a rock-climbing area in Highmoor Park, which I learned of on the council Web site. While I recognize the need to provide more things to do for the young people of Dalehill, ❹I believe the proposed site should be reconsidered. Far from being an "unused grassy area", that part of the park is very popular with dog walkers like me. The benches there are frequently used for resting and for eating lunch. ❺I know this as my house is directly opposite the area.

I am sure an alternative location can be found before construction begins.

Regards,

Michael Newton

5月22日

公園緑地部
Dalehill 町議会
21-39 High Road
Dalehill DH5 8UI

ご担当者様、

議会のウェブサイトで知った Highmoor 公園のロッククライミングエリアの計画に
関してお手紙を差し上げております。Dalehill の若者がもっと活動できることを提
供する必要性は私も認めますが、提案されている場所は再検討されるべきだと強く
思います。「利用されていない草地」の状態からは程遠く、公園のその区画は私の
ような犬の散歩をする人々にとても人気があります。そこにあるベンチは休んだり
昼食をとったりするのに頻繁に利用されます。私の家はそのエリアの真向かいにあ
るので、このことが分かるのです。

建設が始まる前に場所の代替案を見つけられると確信しています。

ではよろしくお願いいたします。

Michael Newton

語句

☐ To whom it may concern: 担当者の方へ　☐ regarding 〜に関して
☐ while 〜である一方で　☐ recognize 〜を認める　☐ need 必要性
☐ believe 〜だと強く思う　☐ propose 〜を提案する　☐ site 場所
☐ reconsider 〜を再考する　☐ far from 〜から遠い
☐ dog walker 犬の散歩をする人　☐ like 〜のような　☐ frequently しばしば
☐ rest 休憩する　☐ as 〜なので　☐ directly opposite 〜の真向かい
☐ I am sure 〜を確信している　☐ alternative 代わりの　☐ location 場所
☐ regards よろしくお願いします

Young Citizens Delighted With New Facility

❻(October 24)—Highmoor Park was buzzing with excitement yesterday as the mayor formally opened a new rock-climbing area. The outdoor facility consists of a four-meter high and 35-meter long wall with various hand grips to grab onto. On its first day, over one hundred people enjoyed testing their skills. ❼While most were youngsters, there were quite a few adults having a <u>go</u>, too.

Community youth worker Annabel Brines couldn't be happier, saying, "This is a great way to get not only young people, but all citizens to exercise and enjoy the outdoors."

新しい施設に喜ぶ市の若者たち

（10月24日）―市長が新しいロッククライミングエリアをついに正式にオープンし、昨日 Highmoor 公園は興奮に沸きました。このアウトドア施設は高さ4メートル、全長35メートルの壁と、つかんで登るために取り付けられた様々なハンドグリップで構成されます。初日には100人以上の人々が自身のスキルを試して楽しみました。大部分は若者たちでしたが、かなり多くの大人たちも挑戦しに来ていました。

若い地域従事者の Annabel Brines はこれ以上ない喜びといった様子で、「若者だけでなく、市民全員に運動しアウトドアを楽しんでもらう最高の方法です」と語りました。

┌ 語句 ┐

☐ citizen 市民　☐ delight 〜を喜ばせる　☐ buzz with 〜でにぎわう

☐ excitement 興奮　☐ mayor 市長　☐ formally 正式に　☐ outdoor 外の

☐ consist of 〜から成る　☐ various 様々な　☐ hand grip 手で握る場所

☐ grab つかむ　☐ skill 技能　☐ youngster 若者

☐ quite a few かなりの数の　☐ have a go やってみる

☐ not only A, but B　Aだけでなく B も　☐ exercise 運動する

☐ outdoor 戸外、アウトドア

21. What does the Web page mention about the rock-climbing project?

(A) It is funded by community donations.

(B) It was the idea of local volunteers.

(C) The cost of tickets is expected to rise.

(D) It cannot be used on certain days.

ウェブページで、ロッククライミング計画について何が分かりますか。

(A) 地域の寄付によって資金を得ている。

(B) 地域のボランティアのアイディアだった。

(C) チケット料金は値上げが予想される。

(D) 特定の日に利用できない。

正解 B

解説

1つ目の文書（ウェブページ）の第1段落の❶に、The proposals were submitted by unpaid community youth leaders「この提案は、無給の地域の若いリーダーたちによって提出されました」とあります。unpaid community youth leaders「無給の地域の若いリーダーたち」を local volunteers「地域のボランティア」に言い換えて表している (B) が正解です。

❶本文→選択肢の言い換え

unpaid community youth leaders ➡ local volunteers

語句
- □ mention ～を述べる　□ fund ～に資金を提供する　□ donation 寄付
- □ local 地元の　□ volunteer ボランティアの人
- □ be expected to do ～することが予想される　□ rise 上がる
- □ certain ある特定の

One-up 貢献と寄付を表す表現

donation は「寄付」を表す名詞で、donate は「〜を寄付する」という他動詞です。donate A to B で「A を B に寄付する」という頻出表現になります。また、contribution は「寄付」「貢献」「寄稿」を表す名詞で、動詞 contribute は、他動詞だと contribute A to B「A を B に寄付する」「A を B に寄稿する」、自動詞だと contribute to「〜に寄付をする」「〜に貢献する」という使い方が頻出です。

22. What is the purpose of the letter?

(A) To criticize a proposal
(B) To request further information
(C) To suggest ideas for activities
(D) To submit a report of citizens' views

この手紙の目的は何ですか。

(A) 提案を批判すること
(B) 詳しい情報を求めること
(C) 活動のためのアイディアを提案すること
(D) 市民の意見の報告書を提出すること

正解 **A**

解説

2 つ目の文書の第 1 段落の❹で、手紙の書き手の Newton さんは I believe the proposed site should be reconsidered「提案されている場所は再検討されるべきだと強く思います」と述べています。その後に続く内容からも、彼は 1 つ目の文書にあるロッククライミング施設を建設する場所の変更を求めていることが分かるため、正解は (A) です。

❶本文→選択肢の言い換え

the proposed site should be reconsidered

    ➡ criticize a proposal

23. What is most likely true about Mr. Newton?

(A) He used to work in construction.

(B) He is an experienced rock climber.

(C) He is head of a local club.

(D) He lives on Jacob Street.

Newton 氏について正しいと思われることは何ですか。

(A) 彼はかつて建設業で働いていた。

(B) 彼は熟練のロッククライマーである。

(C) 彼は地元のクラブの代表である。

(D) 彼は Jacob Street 沿いに住んでいる。

正解　**D**

解説

1つ目の文書の第1段落の❷に、It will be built on an unused grassy area bordering Jacob Street.「それは Jacob Street に隣接する、利用されていない草地に建てられる予定です」とあります。主語の It は前述の an all-weather rock-climbing facility「全天候型ロッククライミング施設」です。また、2つ目の文書（Newton さんが書いた手紙）の第1段落の❺に、I know this as my house is directly opposite the area.「私の家はそのエリアの真向かいにあるので、このことが分かるのです」とあります。the area はロッククライミング施設の建設予定地のことを指すため、Newton さんは Jacob Street 沿いに住んでいることが分かります。よって、正解は（D）です。

❶本文→選択肢の言い換え

my house is directly opposite the area (=bordering Jacob Street)
➡ lives on Jacob Street

語句

☐ used to do 昔は〜していた　☐ experienced　経験豊富な
☐ rock climber　ロッククライマー　☐ head　代表

One-up 「複数文書参照型」問題の解答法

1 度登場した話題が再度登場した時に、それら 2 カ所の話題を関連付けて解答
するのが「複数文書参照型」の問題です。1 つ目の文書に書いてあることと同じ
ことが 2 つ目の文書や 3 つ目の文書に書いてあることに気付いた時点で、「リン
ク（繋がり）を見つけた」と意識します。2 つ目の文書に書いてあることが 3 つ
目の文書に書いてある場合も同様に「リンクを見つけた」と意識してください。
1 つの文書の中でも、この「リンク」を使って解答しなければならないものがあ
ることも、併せて押さえましょう。

24. What problem did the facility encounter?

(A) Bad weather during construction
(B) A delay in opening
(C) A resistance to entrance fees
(D) Overcrowding on the wall

この施設はどのような問題に直面しましたか。

(A) 建設時の悪天候
(B) オープンの遅れ
(C) 入場料への反対
(D) 壁での人の混雑

正解 B

1つ目の文書の第2段落❸に the climbing wall is expected to be open to the public at the end of September「クライミング用の壁は9月末に一般に向けてオープンする予定です」とあり、3つ目の文書の冒頭❻には (October 24) — Highmoor Park was buzzing with excitement yesterday as the mayor formally opened a new rock-climbing area.「(10月24日) －市長が新しいロッククライミングエリアをついに正式にオープンし、昨日 Highmoor 公園は興奮に沸きました」とあります。元々は9月末にオープン予定だったロッククライミングエリアでしたが、実際にオープンしたのは10月23日（記事が書かれた10月24日の前日）となったため、正解は (B) です。

語句

□ encounter ～に直面する　□ during ～の間　□ delay 遅れ
□ resistance 抵抗　□ entrance fee 入場料金　□ overcrowding 密集

One-up　理由を表す接続詞と前置詞句

「～なので」、「～のせいで」のように、理由を表す接続詞として代表的なのは because ですが、同じように使える接続詞、前置詞句を、ここでまとめて押さえておきましょう。

接続詞：① because ② as ③ since ④ for
＊ for は2つの節を並べたときに、必ず2つ目の節の先頭に付きます

前置詞句：① because of ② on account of ③ due to ④ owing to
　　　　　⑤ thanks to

25. In the article, the word "go" in paragraph 1, line 5, is closest in meaning to

(A) attempt
(B) permission
(C) recommendation
(D) journey

記事の第1段落・5行目にある "go" に最も意味が近いのは

(A) 試み
(B) 許可
(C) 推薦
(D) 旅

正解 **A**

解説

単語の言い換え問題です。3つ目の文書の第1段落の❼に、While most were youngsters, there were quite a few adults having a go, too.「大部分は若者たちでしたが、かなり多くの大人たちも挑戦しに来ていました」とあります。have a go には「やってみる」という意味があるため、正解は（A）の attempt「試み」です。have an attempt to do だと「〜するのを試みる」という意味になります。

語句
☐ paragraph 段落　☐ be closest in meaning to 〜に意味が最も近い

Chapter

2

Part 7 の概要と攻略法

1 | Part 7 の概要

- **Part 7 で出題される典型的なタイプの文書を知る**
- **「どこに何が書かれているのか」を覚える**

この2つにより、Part 7 に登場するほぼ全ての問題文を読解して解答できるようになります。

Part 7 に登場する主な問題文（＝文書）のタイプは様々ですが、主に以下のようなものが出題されます。

出題される典型的なタイプの文書

① E メール（e-mail）
② 手紙（letter）
③ 記事（article）
④ 報告書（report）
⑤ 広告（advertisement）
⑥ 案内（information）
⑦ お知らせ（notice）
⑧ メモ・社内回覧（memo）
⑨ ウェブページ（Web page、Web site）
⑩ 指示書・取扱説明書（instructions）
⑪ 領収書（receipt）
⑫ 請求書（invoice）
⑬ スケジュール（schedule）
⑭ 旅程表（itinerary）
⑮ 申込用紙（form）
⑯ アンケート（survey）
⑰ オンラインチャット（text-message chain、online chat discussion）
⑱ 複数の文書（multiple passages）

　Part 7 の問題文の最初に、Questions XXX-XXX refer to the following ○○. とあり、この○○の部分に、問題文の文書の種類が入ります。

　　例：Questions 147-148 refer to the following notice.

　　　　（問題 147-148 は次のお知らせに関するものです。）

　⑱の multiple passages の問題の○○のところには、2 つの文書の問題であれば e-mail and article、3 つの文書の問題であれば Web page, letter, and article のように記されます。

　　例：Questions 191-195 refer to the following Web page, letter, and article.

　　　　（問題 191-195 は次のウェブページ、手紙、記事に関するものです。）

　左記以外のタイプの文書も TOEIC L&R テストには登場しますが、これに関してはあまり神経質になりすぎる必要はありません。

　社内回覧や報告書などの、ビジネスで使われる文書だけでなく、私たちが普段の生活で目にするありとあらゆるタイプの文書が登場します。

　ですが、左ページに挙げた「出題される典型的なタイプの文書」を押さえ、「どこに何が書かれているのか」を覚えることにより、Part 7 に登場するほぼ全ての問題文を読解して解答できるようになるはずです。

設問タイプ

　Part 7 に登場する主な設問（意図問題、位置問題、言い換え問題以外）をここで確認しておきましょう。

　設問は大きく次の 3 つのタイプに分けられます。

> ① ピンポイント情報について問う設問
> ② 問題文全体について問う設問
> ③ NOT 問題

　それぞれの設問タイプについて具体例を見ていきましょう。

よりぬき！テスト

解説

攻略法

トレーニング

確認テスト

解説

トレーニング

① ピンポイント情報について問う設問

1. What is suggested about the invoice?
請求書について何が示唆されていますか。

2. What is Ms. Hayasaka asked to do?
ハヤサカさんは何をするよう求められていますか。

3. When will the discount be applied to the merchandise?
いつ割引は商品に適用されますか。

4. Where does Mr. Naito work?
ナイトウさんはどこで働いていますか。

5. Who most likely is Hiromu?
ヒロムはおそらく誰ですか。

6. Who will be surveyed?
誰が調査対象ですか。

7. What is true about Mr. Sanada?
サナダさんについて正しいものはどれですか。

8. According to the notice, what will occur this weekend?
お知らせによれば、今週末何が起こりますか。

9. At what time will the flower shop open during the summer?
夏の間、花屋は何時に開店しますか。

10. What is available in the London location?
ロンドンの店舗では何が入手できますか。

11. What is offered to those who purchased an electric chain saw?
電動のこぎりを買った人は何がもらえますか。

12. When will the interview take place?
面接はいつ行われますか。

13. When is the deadline for the report to be submitted?
レポートの提出期限はいつですか。

14. How often should the light bulbs be replaced?
どのくらいの頻度で電球は交換されるべきですか。

15. For how long has Mr. Watanabe stayed in the U.S.?
ワタナベさんはどのくらいの間アメリカに滞在していますか。

16. Where will the conference be held?
どこで会議は開催されますか。

ピンポイント情報について問う設問は、<u>問題文のある特定の部分を読めば正解を</u>選ぶことができるタイプの問題です。
<u>ただし、その「特定の部分」を探し出すために飛ばし読みをすることなく読み進</u>めていき、設問に対する<u>「正解の根拠はここだ」と思える前後数行の内容</u>も踏まえて解答するようにすることが肝要です。

② 問題文全体について問う設問

1. What is the purpose of the letter?
手紙の目的は何ですか。

2. What is the subject of the memo?
メモの主題は何ですか。

3. Why was the e-mail written?
なぜ E メールは書かれましたか。

これらは問題文の「目的」や「主題」、もしくは問題文が書かれた「理由」を問う設問です。
問題文全体をきちんと読んで理解する必要があります。
<u>多くの場合、問題文にある語句と同じ語句を使って作られている選択肢は引っか</u>けとなっています。
問題文に書かれていることを集約し、<u>「抽象的」、「一般的」な表現に言い換えている</u>ものが正解になる場合が多いです。

また、上記のパターン以外にも、一見「ピンポイント情報について問う設問」に見える「問題文全体について問う設問」もあります。
いくつか例を見てみましょう。

4. What does the Web page explain?
ウェブページは何を説明していますか。

5. What type of business is LIJ co.?
LIJ 社は何の会社ですか。

よりぬき！テスト

解説

攻略法

トレーニング

確認テスト

解説

トレーニング

6. **For whom is this memo most likely intended?**
   このメモは誰に向けられていると考えられますか。

7. **What will be discussed at the today's meeting?**
   今日の会議では何について話し合われますか。

8. **What product will be reviewed?**
   何の商品がレビューされますか。

9. **Where would the article most likely appear?**
   記事はどこに掲載されていると考えられますか。

10. **What is being described on the Web site?**
    ウェブサイトには何が書かれていますか。

11. **What is being advertised?**
    何が宣伝されていますか。

12. **Where would the notice most likely appear?**
    このお知らせはどこに載る可能性が高いですか。

これらの設問は、一見具体的なことを問う設問に見えますが、「問題文の内容を広く理解する必要がある」という意味で、「問題文全体について問う問題」であると考えることができます。

③ NOT 問題

1. **What does Mr. Okada NOT offer to provide?**
   オカダさんが提供を申し出ていないものはどれですか。

2. **What is NOT stated about the Big Peach Airlines?**
   Big Peach Airlines について述べられていないものはどれですか。

3. **What is NOT advertised in today's newspaper?**
   今日の新聞で宣伝されていないのはどれですか。

4. **What is NOT enclosed in the letter?**
   手紙に同封されていないものはどれですか。

NOT 問題は、設問の中に「大文字の NOT」が含まれているものです。
NOT 問題の正解となる選択肢の内容は、他の問題とは違って、正解を選ぶための情報が問題文の中には登場しません。

　NOT 問題を解く際は、誤答の根拠を 3 つ、問題文の中から探します。

　上記 1. の設問 What does Mr. Okada NOT offer to provide?（オカダさんが提供を申し出ていないものはどれですか）を例にとると、「オカダさんが提供を申し出ているもの」を 3 つ探すのです。

　誤答の根拠を 3 つ探し終えた時点で、残った選択肢を正解としてマークしてください。

> 　**NOT 問題は「ピンポイント情報について問う設問」× 3 問分を解答**するのと同じ労力を要することになるので、必然的に解答時間が余計にかかります。
>
> 　ですが、**選択肢を先に読んで理解**しておき、問題文を読み進めていく中で**「選択肢の内容と一致すること」が登場するたびに一つひとつ選択肢を消していく**ようにすれば、意外と容易に解答することが可能であるということを押さえておいてください。

　これら①〜③以外に登場する 3 つのパターン（意図問題、位置問題、言い換え問題）についても、実際にどのように出題されるのかを見ておきましょう。

・意図問題

　オンラインチャット（text-message chain、online chat discussion）タイプの問題において、以下のように出題されます。

> **At 11:23 A.M., what does Mr. Naito most likely mean when he writes, "It's good enough"?**
> 午前 11 時 23 分にナイトウさんが "It's good enough" と書く際、何を意図していると考えられますか。

　意図問題は、設問の中に「ダブルクォーテーションに挟まれた短い発言」があります。

　この発言がされているチャットの前後の文脈をしっかりと押さえ、この発言の出た「状況」、「背景」を理解して正解を選ぶようにします。

・位置問題

　長めの文書の中に 4 箇所の [空所] があり、提示された文を入れるのに適切な箇所

よりぬきⅠテスト

解説

攻略法

トレーニング

確認テスト

解説

トレーニング

を選ぶ問題で、以下のように出題されます。

> **In which of the positions marked [1], [2], [3] and [4] does the following sentence best belong?**
>
> ［1］、［2］、［3］、［4］と記載された箇所のうち、次の文が入るのに最もふさわしいのはどれですか。

　上記にある設問に続いて、問題文に挿入すべき1文が提示されます。

　このタイプの問題も意図問題と同様、文脈を理解し、提示された文と「そこでの話題」が合うものを選ぶようにします。

　前後関係や順序を表す接続詞や副詞などに注意して解答するのがコツとなります。

・言い換え問題

　問題文中の単語・語句とほぼ同じ意味の選択肢を選ぶ問題で、以下のように出題されます。

> **In the article, the word "store" in paragraph 3, line 2 is closest in meaning to**
>
> 記事の第3段落・2行目にある "store" に最も意味が近いのは

　言い換え問題は多くの場合、設問にある単語・語句（上の例であれば store）が含まれている1文を読むだけで解答することが可能です。

　選択肢には4つの単語・語句が並びますが、単体同士で同じ意味になる類義語を選ぶのではなく、設問にある単語・語句がその文の中ではどのような意味で使われているのかを理解し、それに最も意味が近いものを選ぶようにして解答してください。

　例えば上の例にある store が入っている例文が以下だったとします。

　　We should know how to store the food.

　この場合、store は「〜を保存する」という意味で使われているので、preserve や house のような単語とほぼ同じ意味で使われていることが分かります。

　また、指定される単語・語句は「やさしめの多義語」であることが多いのですが、「甘く見ないこと」、「単なる類義語を選ばないこと」を意識して解答するようにしてください。

タイムマネジメント

Part 7 では全部で 54 問の問題が出題されます。

リーディングセクションは全 100 問を 75 分で解答しなくてはいけませんが、900 点前後〜990 点満点を取る人たちでも、最後まで解答し終えるのは簡単なことではありません。

以下のペースでリーディングセクションを解き進めて行けば、理論上は時間内に全ての問題を解き終えることが可能です。

Part 5
全 30 問を 10 分以内に解答

1 問平均 20 秒 × 30 問 = 600 秒 = **10 分**

Part 6
全 16 問を 8 分以内に解答

1 問平均 30 秒 × 16 問 = 480 秒 = **8 分**

上記のペースで Part 5 と Part 6 の問題に解答すれば、持ち時間 75 分 − 18 分 = **57 分**の時間が Part 7 に残ります。

Part 7
全 54 問を 57 分以内に解答

1 問平均 1 分 × 54 問 = **54 分**（3 分余り）

Part 7 に関しては、1 問当たり平均 1 分で解答しなくてはなりませんが、これはなかなかのスピードが要求される制限時間です。

例えば 1 つの文書に 4 つの設問が付いているセットであれば、4 分でそれらを解き終える、ということです。

解くのに時間がかかる難しめの設問もあれば、早く解き終えることのできるやさしめの設問もあります。

なので、1 問を 1 分で解くことにはこだわらず、1 セットを「セットに含まれる問題数 × 1 分」で解答することを目標とし、「Part 7 全部の問題を 54 分以内に解く」ことを最終的な目標にしてみてください。

解く速さにこだわるのは大切ですが、まずは自分のペースで内容を確実に理解し

よりぬき！テスト

解 説

攻略法

トレーニング

確認テスト

解 説

トレーニング

つつ読み進めることができるようになることを優先してください。

　解答時間が足りないからといって、決して問題文の飛ばし読みをしたりしてはいけません。

　語彙力や文法力を高めていくと同時に、長文を大量に読んで**「読むことに慣れる」**ことが大切です。

「知識の蓄積」と「長文を読むことに対する慣れ」が、読解速度と解答精度をアップさせてくれるのです。

読解スピードを上げるためにやるべきこと

1. 自分の解答速度を知りましょう

　ストップウオッチを用意してください。

　まずは時間を意識せず、問題文をしっかりと「精読」優先で読むようにします。

　そして問題を解き、そのセットの解答時間がどのくらいかかっているのかを記録します。

　1問平均1分以内に解答できるのが理想的なので、1つの文書につき3問の問題が付いているセットであれば、3分以内に全て解き終えることができると良いでしょう。

　自分の解答速度がどのくらいなのかを把握してください。

2. マイナス○○秒を意識して問題に取り組みましょう

　3問付きのセットの問題を全て解答するのに3分40秒かかった場合は、40秒の短縮を目標とする必要があります。

　自分がどのくらい時間を短縮するべきなのかを理解するようにします。

3. 復習＋再解答をします

　理解をするのに時間がかかった部分、理解をすることができなかった表現や文は、解説をきちんと読んで理解し、それを踏まえてもう一度同じ問題を解くようにします。

　英文の内容も問題の正解も分かった上での再解答ですが、ここで大切なのは以下の3つです。

　① 全ての設問、選択肢、そして本文の全ての文を『英語のままで』理解できる
　　状態であること

② 上から下まで、1文たりとも飛ばさずに英文を読解すること

③ 初見の問題を解くのと同じ手順で各問題を『本番さながらに』解答すること

　一度解いて内容も正解も分かってしまった問題（文）に対して、今度はそれをどこまで「**自分のストック**」にできるかが読解力と読解スピードの向上につながるカギです。

　正しく英文を読みつつ速読力を上げる方法は、「完璧に理解できているセット」を「本番さながらに解答する」、を繰り返すことです。

　これを行うことにより、「自分の最高速度で完璧に英語を英語のまま理解できるセット」が自分の中にストックされていきます。

　初見の問題を速く正確に読解できるかどうかは、この「**ストックの数**」に正比例します。

　ストックの数が多ければ多いほど、初見の問題でも読みやすく、解きやすくなるのです。

　初見の英文が読めるということは、その英文で使われている単語や語句が自分の頭の中にストックされているからであり、その英文で使われている文法事項、構文のパターンをストックできているからです。

　本書のトレーニングを全て終えた後、まずは『公式 TOEIC Listening & Reading 問題集』1冊分に入っている2つの模試の内、片方（模試1回分）に収録されている Part 7 の 15 セットの問題全てを自分のストックにすることをお勧めします。

2 | Part 7（読解問題）の攻略法

「ベタ読み」でしっかりと英文を理解しつつ読み進めていく

　本書では基本的に、英文を飛ばし読みではなく全て読む「**ベタ読み**」をお勧めします。

　いや、お勧めではなく、「**必ず全ての英文を読む**」ようにしてください。

　Part 7 の英文の量は非常に多いため、ともすると飛ばし読みを勧めるようなアドバイスすら見かけます。

　ですが、それではいつまでたっても「速く正確に読める」日はやってきません。

　リーディングセクションの制限時間は 75 分ですが、その時間内に Part 5 と Part 6 の問題に全て解答し、Part 7 の英文を全て読みきって理解した上で解答し終えることを目標にしてほしいのです。

　ちなみに、900 点を取得しているような人はもちろんのこと、990 点満点を取得したことがあるような人ですら、リーディングセクションの 100 問を 75 分の制限時間内に解き終えることができなかった、ということはざらにあります。

　それでも本書では、全ての英文をきちんと読む、上から下まで隈なく読む「ベタ読み」を勧めます。

　それこそが「文脈をきちんと正しく理解すること」につながる最良の方法だからです。

　左から右に、返り読みすることなく英文を読み進めることを常としてください。

　読解スピードは後からついてきます。

　「**同じ英文を何回も繰り返し読むこと**」、そして「**語彙や文法の知識の量が増えること**」により、英文を読むスピードは上がってきます。

Part 7 の基本的な解答手順

Part 7 の問題の解答手順の基本は以下になります。

1. 1つ目の設問を読んで記憶し、問題文を読み進めていく

まず問題文を読む前に、1つ目の設問を先読みし、記憶します。

設問を記憶する際は、内容を要約して頭の片隅に保持します。これを本書では「**要約リテンション**」と呼びます。

設問例：What is suggested about the occupants of Room 204?

この設問であれば「Room 204 何が分かる？」と要約リテンションします。

設問は大きく以下の2つのパターンに分かれます。

① ピンポイント型

→ 設問を記憶し、問題文を読み進めていく過程で、正解の根拠が見つかり次第解答できるタイプの問題

(例) What problem did the Leytons encounter?

問題文を読み進めていく中で、Leyton が出くわした「問題（良くないこと）」にたどり着いた時点で、選択肢とそれを照合して解答することが可能です。

② 内容一致型

→ 問題文を読み進めていく中で、どこが正解の根拠となるのかが判断しづらいタイプの問題

(例) What is indicated about the hotel?

問題文全体がホテルについて書かれている場合、問題文のどこが正解のヒントとなるのかを判断することは容易ではありません。

Part 7 では、②内容一致型の出題の方が多いと認識しておいてください。

2. 解答するタイミングは 2 パターン

　① 設問を読んで問題文を読み進めていき、正解の根拠が見つかった場合には、その時点で選択肢へと進みます。
　正解の根拠と思える部分と一致する選択肢を正解として選びマークします。
　ピンポイント型の設問はこのタイミングで解答することができます。

　② 内容一致型の設問の場合には、問題文を最後まで読み進めた上で選択肢へと進みます。
　問題文に書かれていたことをきちんと記憶できているかどうかが正解を選ぶカギとなります。
　問題文の内容と一致する選択肢を正解として選びマークします。
　その際、問題文に書かれていたことに対して「記憶に自信がない」場合でも、選択肢の内容と一致することが書かれていた（問題文の）場所に、間髪入れず戻って内容を確認するクセをつけてください。
　限られた時間を最大限有効に活用するためにも、設問と問題文に関しては常に「できる限り記憶する」つもりで読むようにします。

3. 正解を選んだら、次の設問へと進みます

　前の問題が内容一致型の場合、この時点ですでに問題文を読み終えていることとなります。
　設問を読んだ時点ですべきことは次の 2 パターンのいずれかです。

　① 選択肢に進み、問題文の内容の記憶を頼りに正解を選んでマークする

　② 選択肢に進み、正解だと思える選択肢を確認し、その選択肢に書かれていることと一致する（問題文中の）箇所に戻り、正解だと確認した上でそれをマークする

　上記の 1.〜3. を繰り返し、そのセットの問題に全て解答したらタスク終了、次のセットへと進みます。

問題文のタイプごとに読み方を変える

問題文のタイプは大きく分けて3つです。

基本は「ベタ読み」ですが、問題文のタイプによっては「読まなくてもいい部分」もあります。

以下にタイプごとの例を挙げるので、「読まなくてもいい部分」、「注意すべき部分」を知っておいてください。

1. Eメール、手紙など

問題文のほぼ全てがセンテンスから成っています。

このパターンの問題文は、基本的に全て読むようにしてください。

ただし、以下の箇所はきちんと読まなくても大丈夫な場合が多いです。

① Eメールの @（アットマーク）の前

@ の前は、多くの場合そのメールアカウントを持っている人の名前となっています。

送信者の名前は別に書かれているので、この部分を読む必要はありません。

ただし、@ 以下の部分（ドメイン）は、その人の「所属先」となっている場合が多いので、ここは必ず「見て確認」するようにしてください。

（Eメールの例）

From: Stanley Berg <sberg@ewaveburger.com>

この場合、Eメールアドレスの@の前にある sberg は Stanley Berg さんのことで、読む必要はなく、@以下の ewaveburger.com を確認します（E-Wave Burger の人だと分かる）。

② 手紙の住所の中にある数字や電話番号

住所の中にある「地名」は重要ですが、数字や記号、URL や電話番号などは、読むのではなく「見る」だけで十分です。

（住所の例）

21-39 High Road

Dalehill DH5 8UI

よりぬき！テスト

解説

攻略法

トレーニング

確認テスト

解説

トレーニング

この場合、High Road と Dalehill だけを読み、他の部分は読まずに目視だけします。

（URL と電話番号の例）
www.tomtombakery.com
555-0990

上記のような URL や電話番号は、いずれも読む必要はありません。

2. リスト形式の図表

リスト形式の図表には、カンファレンスのタイムテーブルや、職場の勤務シフト表などがあります。

このタイプの図表では、「必要な部分を読む」だけで、解答するのにこと足りる場合が多いです。

3. テキストメッセージとオンラインチャットの問題

Part 7 の全 15 セットのうち 2 セット、スマホやパソコン、タブレット上での複数人によるやりとりが行われている画面が問題として出題されます。

これらのタイプの問題では、時刻の部分は意図問題を解く際に確認として使用するだけです。

また、登場人物が 2 名以上出てきますのでそちらに意識が向いてしまいがちですが、あくまでも大事なのは「やりとりの内容」です。

各人の発言をきちんと繋ぎながら追うようにし、文脈を理解することを最優先して解答します。

3 | 英文の読み方（左から右に）

スラッシュリーディングとは（概要と効果）

　Part 7 の問題を解くためには、大量の英文を短時間で読みこなさなくてはなりません。

　Part 7 の文書は、ある程度の英文読解力があれば、決して難易度は高くはありません。

　ですが、制限時間に対して読まなければならない量が、ほとんどの方々にとって過剰なのです。

　900 点という高得点を取るような人でも、Part 7 の問題を最後まで解き終えることができないということはざらにあります。

　ここでは英文を読むための基本戦略として、**スラッシュリーディング**（区切り読み）を身に付けることをお勧めします。

　問題文を読む際は、**きれいな日本語に訳そうとしてはいけません。**

　英語と日本語は語順が全く異なるので、日本語に訳しながら読もうとすると、どうしても後ろから前に返り読みをしなくてはならなくなり、余計な時間がかかってしまいます。

　では、以下に「日本語の語順に直して理解する」パターンと、「英語の語順のまま理解する」パターンを紹介します。

　どちらの方が早く読めるでしょうか。

　まずは「日本語の語順に直して理解する」パターンです。

If you wish towels to be replaced during room cleaning, please place used towels on the bathroom floor.

「もしあなたが部屋の清掃中にタオルの交換を望むのであれば、バスルームの床に使用済みのタオルを置いておいてください」

このようなきれいな日本語に訳して理解した場合、英文を以下の順序で読むことになります。

① If you / ⑤ wish / ③ towels / ④ to be replaced / ② during room cleaning, / ⑧ please place / ⑦ used towels / ⑥ on the bathroom floor.

この読み方だと、英文を左から右に読み、また左に戻る、ということを繰り返すため、すでに読む必要のない部分の上を複数回に渡って視線をやる必要が出てきてしまいます。

次に「英語の語順のまま理解する」パターンです。

もしあなたが / 望むなら / タオルの / 交換を / 部屋の清掃中に、/ 置いておいてください / 使用済みのタオルを / バスルームの床に

英語の語順のまま理解したため、英文を以下の順序で読むことになります。

① If you / ② wish / ③ towels / ④ to be replaced / ⑤ during room cleaning, / ⑥ please place / ⑦ used towels / ⑧ on the bathroom floor.

このように読んでいくことで、英文を左から右へと一方通行で理解することができるため、返り読みを避けることができます。
同時に「きれいな日本語訳を作ろう」という作業もしなくてよくなるため、よりスピーディーに英文を読解できるようになります。

スラッシュリーディングができるようになると、リスニング力も格段にアップします。
リスニングは英語を語順通りに理解する必要があるので、まさにスラッシュリーディングと同じことをリスニングでは行っているからです。

スラッシュリーディングをやるための準備

では、実際どのように英文を区切れば良いのかを説明していきましょう。

If you wish towels to be replaced during room cleaning, please place used towels on the bathroom floor.

　これが元の文ですが、まずは文の要素で区切ってみます。
　文の要素とは以下のものを指します。

・主語
　その文の中心となる名詞のことです。
　本書では the bath room floor のような名詞句（名詞のカタマリ）も名詞と呼ぶことにしています。
　主語の後ろで英文を区切ります。

・動詞
　述語の先頭となり、主語の説明をします。
　本書では動詞、現在完了形の have ＋過去分詞、助動詞＋動詞の原形、動詞＋不定詞、動詞＋現在分詞、受動態などの動詞句（動詞のカタマリ）も動詞と表しています。
　動詞の前後で英文を区切ります。

・目的語
　動詞の動作の対象となる名詞のことです。
　目的語の前で英文を区切ります。

・補語
　主語や目的語を説明する名詞や形容詞のことです。
　補語の前で英文を区切ります。

　文の要素で上記の英文を区切ると、以下のようになります。

主語　　動詞　　　　目的語　　　　　　　　　　　　　　　　　　　　　　　動詞
If you / wish / towels to be replaced during room cleaning, please place /
　　目的語
used towels on the bathroom floor.

　文の要素の前後で区切るだけでも、すでに英文を前から読むことが容易になりました。
　さらに以下の要素で区切ってみます。

よりぬき！テスト

解説

攻略法

トレーニング

確認テスト

解説

トレーニング

・カンマの後ろ

・接続詞の前

・関係詞の前

・前置詞の前（句動詞のように他の語とセットで使われるものを除く）

・to 不定詞の前

・副詞 (句) の前後

・時を表すカタマリの前後（前置詞の前や副詞 (句) の前後と重複します）

・場所を表すカタマリの前後（前置詞の前や副詞 (句) の前後と重複します）

| to 不定詞の前 | 時を表すカタマリの前 | | カンマの後ろ |

If you / wish / towels / to be replaced / during room cleaning, / please place /

| 場所を表すカタマリの前 |

used towels / on the bathroom floor.

　これで以下のように英文を前から順番に理解していくことができるはずです。

もしあなたが / 望むなら / タオルの / 交換を / 部屋の清掃中に、/ 置いておいてください / 使用済みのタオルを / バスルームの床に

スラッシュリーディングの練習

　スラッシュリーディングをやるための準備が整ったら、以下の手順で練習します。

STEP 1
英文の意味を左から右に、区切られた順番通りに言ってみる

If you / wish / towels / to be replaced / during room cleaning, / please place / used towels / on the bathroom floor.

左から順番通りに意味を言う
もしあなたが / 望むなら / タオルの / 交換を / 部屋の清掃中に / 置いておいてください / 使用済みのタオルを / バスルームの床に

　訳せない部分があれば、辞書や参考書などを使って必ず該当箇所の意味を調べるようにします。

　この段階で、英文のどの部分を指されても「英語を見た瞬間に日本語訳が言える」ようにしてください。

　さらに、以下のことを全て確実にクリアするようにします。

- **分からない単語や語句（フレーズ）をきちんと調べる**
  → 単語は意味、品詞、発音をセットで理解し、使い方（例文）まで確認するのが理想です。

- **時制を意識する**
  → 現在形、過去形、未来を表す表現、それらの中にある進行形や完了形を含めて、どれが使われているのかを意識します。

- **態を意識する**
  → 能動態（〜が…する）なのか、受動態（〜が…される）なのか、常に注意を払うようにします。

- **代名詞がある場合には、それが何を指しているのかを意識する**
  → 代名詞は短く簡単な単語ばかりなので無意識に軽視しがちです。「それが何を指しているのか」を常に意識するようにします。

- **修飾語句と被修飾句語句の関係を認識する**
  → 英文中のどの部分がどの部分を修飾しているのかを意識して理解するようにします。

- **関係詞がある場合には先行詞と関係詞節を認識する**
  → 先行詞（名詞）とそれを説明する関係詞節の組み合わせを、意識して認識するようにします。

　また、スラッシュの位置は p.109-110 で挙げた箇所が基本ですが、語句の長さやカタマリの大きさなどによって、ご自身のレベルに合わせて変えてください。

　区切りが細かすぎるとかえって理解しづらくなることもあります。また見慣れたフレーズですぐに理解できるものや、定番表現などは無理に区切る必要はありません。（例：Leave it to me.「任せてください」）

　慣れてくると、区切りを減らしても左から右へ一方通行で読めるようになり、読

むスピードもアップします。

STEP 2
英文を音読する
　英文を見ながら、そして**お手本となる音声を聞きながら**、**音声と同時に英文を音読**します。

　できる限り音声のマネをすることを心掛けてください。

　音声を聞きながら（ヘッドホンやイヤホンを使うことを推奨します）、まずは10回連続で同じ文を音読してください。

　STEP 1の段階で「読んだ瞬間に英語を日本語に訳せる」英文を用意し、その英文をお手本となる音声通りに音読する練習をすることにより、「**英語を英語のまま、英文を左から右へと理解できる**」ということがどういうことなのかを実感することができるはずです。

　音読する回数は「1つの文書につき100回」を目標としてください。

　1日10回同じ英文を音読するのであれば、それを10日間続けます。

　1日20回同じ英文を音読するのであれば、それを5日間続けます。

　これを行うことにより、「英語のまま日本語を介さずに理解することができる」英文が自分の中にストックされていきます。

　初見の英文を英語のまま理解できるかどうかは、ストックしている英文の数と比例します。

　音読トレーニングにより、英文のストックを増やしていくことで、知っている単語や語句、理解できる構文の数が増えていきます。同時に、類似したパターンの英文を即座に理解する力が培われていきます。

　焦らず着実に、一つひとつ英文をモノにしていきましょう。

トレーニング

よりぬき！テストで
スラッシュリーディングと音読

4 | トレーニング
英文をストックする

スラッシュリーディングを身に付ける

　前にも述べたように、英文を速く読めるようになるためには、初見の英文に多く取り組むのではなく、同じ英文を繰り返しトレーニングに使うことが大事です。

　使われている語彙や文法事項を確認し、内容を理解した上で、英語の語順のまま理解できるようになれば、自分の中にストックされていきます。そのストックを増やすことで、初見の英文を読むスピードも上がっていくのです。

　ここからは、英文のストックを増やしていくための実践トレーニングです。

　Chapter1 の「よりぬき！テスト」を活用して、スラッシュリーディングを身に付けましょう。

　次ページから、「よりぬき！テスト」の問題文を返り読みできないように改行したスラッシュリーディングトレーニング用のテキストを掲載しています。

　スラッシュリーディングで、英語の語順で読み進めて行く感覚を身に付けてください。

　区切りの箇所は参考に入れていますが、ご自身のレベルに応じて変えていただいてかまいません。

　ですが、必ず**「左から右へ一方通行で読む」**ことを心掛けましょう。

　p.111 で示したように、訳せない部分があれば辞書や参考書などで調べて確実にクリアするようにし、**「英語を見た瞬間に日本語訳を言える」**ようにします。

英文を音読する

　スラッシュリーディングで「英語の語順のまま理解できる」ようになったら、今度はその英文の「音読」を繰り返すことにより、確実に自分のものにしていきます。

　「よりぬき！テスト」問題文の音声を用意しましたので、スラッシュリーディングのトレーニングの後は、音声を聞き、お手本のまねをして音読してみましょう。

よりぬき！テスト

解　説

攻略法

トレーニング

確認テスト

解　説

トレーニング

　音声は、当然ですが必ず「左から右へ一方通行」です。スラッシュリーディングで身に付けた「英語の語順で理解する」ことを、音読を通して実感し、強化していきます。

　また、いちいち「この英語の意味はなんだっけ…」などと考えている時間はありません。そのためにも、先にしっかり「読んだ瞬間に英語を日本語に訳せる」状態にしてから音読練習に取り組むことが大事です。

　これを繰り返すことにより、**英語を英語のまま理解できるようになり、そのストックを増やしていくことで、長文読解のスピードが上がっていきます。**

スラッシュリーディング　トレーニング ①

Questions 1-2 / refer to / the following notice.
問題 1-2 は / 〜に関するものです / 次のお知らせ

Guest Notice　客へのお知らせ
Room number: 204　部屋番号：204
Date: July 19　日付：7 月 19 日
Cleaning crew:　A B C　清掃担当者：B

Your room　あなたの部屋は
☐ was cleaned　清掃された
☑ was not cleaned / because　清掃されなかった / なぜなら

☐ you requested / no cleaning　あなたが依頼した / 清掃不要
☑ the room was / constantly occupied　部屋が〜だった / ずっと使用中

Fresh towels are　新しいタオルはある
☐ in your bathroom　バスルームに
☑ available / upon request　利用できる / 依頼に応じて

If you / wish / towels　もしあなたが / 希望するなら / タオルを
to be replaced　交換されるのを
during room cleaning,　部屋の清掃の間に

115

please place / used towels　置いてください / 使用済みのタオルを

on the bathroom floor.　バスルームの床に

This helps / avoid unnecessary waste　これは助ける / 不必要な浪費を避ける

and pollution.　そして汚染を

Alternatively, / guests can contact / reception　または / 客は連絡できる / 受付に

from 11 A.M. to 6 P.M.　午前 11 時から午後 6 時まで

音読 トレーニング ①

Questions 1-2 refer to the following notice.　🎧 Track 01

Guest Notice

Room number: *204*

Date: *July 19*

Cleaning crew:　A (B) C

Your room

☐ was cleaned

☑ was not cleaned because　　☐ you requested no cleaning

　　　　　　　　　　　　　　　☑ the room was constantly
　　　　　　　　　　　　　　　　occupied

Fresh towels are

☐ in your bathroom

☑ available upon request

If you wish towels to be replaced during room cleaning, please place used towels on the bathroom floor. This helps avoid unnecessary waste and pollution. Alternatively, guests can contact reception from 11 A.M. to 6 P.M.

スラッシュリーディング　トレーニング ②

Questions 3-4 / refer to / the following text-massage chain.
問題 3-4 は / 〜に関するものです / 次のテキストメッセージのやりとり

Kenneth Linnehan　Kenneth Linnehan
4:12 P.M.　午後 4 時 12 分
Sally, / have the new chairs and tables　Sally / 新しい椅子とテーブルは
for the lobby　ロビー用の
arrived / yet?　到着しましたか / もう

Sally Ng　Sally Ng
4:15 P.M.　午後 4 時 15 分
Yes.　はい
The other receptionists and I　他の受付の人たちと私は
placed them / in three circles.　それらを置いた / 3 つの円形に
They were / useful　それらは〜だった / 役に立つ
when guests were waiting　客が待っていたときに
to check in / this afternoon.　チェックインする / 今日の午後

Kenneth Linnehan　Kenneth Linnehan
4:16 P.M.　午後 4 時 16 分
That's great.　それは素晴らしい
By the way,　ところで
I forgot / to mention that　私は忘れた / 〜ということを言うのを
two sofas will come / tomorrow.　2 つのソファが来るということ / 明日
You'll need / to make space　あなたは必要がある / スペースを作る
for them / among the chairs.　それらのために / 椅子の間に

Sally Ng　Sally Ng
4:17 P.M.　午後 4 時 17 分
Leave it to me.　お任せください
I'll make sure / everything looks good.　私は確実にやります / 全てが良く見える
ように

Questions 3-4 refer to the following text-message chain.

 Track 02

Kenneth Linnehan   **4:12** P.M.

Sally, have the new chairs and tables for the lobby arrived yet?

Sally Ng   **4:15** P.M.

Yes. The other receptionists and I placed them in three circles. They were useful when guests were waiting to check in this afternoon.

Kenneth Linnehan   **4:16** P.M.

That's great. By the way, I forgot to mention that two sofas will come tomorrow. You'll need to make space for them among the chairs.

Sally Ng   **4:17** P.M.

Leave it to me. I'll make sure everything looks good.

スラッシュリーディング **トレーニング ③**

Questions 5-7 / refer to / the following article.
問題 5-7 は / ～に関するものです / 次の記事

A Company / on the Up　ある会社 / 好調な

Sci-kid Toys / has been getting / a lot of media attention / lately
Sci-kid Toys は / ～を得ている / 多くのメディアの注目 / 最近
for its imaginative science toys and kits.　その独創的な科学玩具とキットで
But success didn't come / immediately　しかし成功はやってこなかった / すぐには
for the company.　その会社にとって

Founders Ron and Amanda Leyton,　創設者の Ron と Amanda Leyton
a married couple / from Inverness,　夫妻 / Inverness からの
became disappointed　落胆した
when looking for / stimulating toys　～を探しているときに / 刺激的なおもちゃ
for their 5-year-old son, Lucas.　彼らの 5 歳になる息子 Lucas のために
"There was nothing　何も無かった
that required / thought or skill",　それは要求した / 考えることや技能を
said Ron.　ロンは言った
So, / three years ago,　それで / 3 年前に
they started / making toys　彼らは始めた / おもちゃを作ることを
with Lucas　Lucas と
using their own ideas.　彼ら自身のアイディアを使って
Amanda explains,　Amanda は説明する
"We used / household objects and wood　私たちは使った / 家庭用の物と木材を
to make moving cars,　動く車を作るために
bottle rockets,　瓶のロケット
and model cranes.　そして模型クレーン
Lucas loved it!"　Lucas はそれが大好きだった

119

Spotting a business opportunity,　ビジネスの機会を見つけて

the pair started / selling instructional booklets　夫妻は始めた / 教本を売ることを

of their toys.　彼らのおもちゃの

However, / the plans were soon copied　しかしながら / そのプランはすぐにまねされた

and shared / over the Internet.　そして共有された / インターネットを通して

After a hard six months　つらい6カ月間の後

of little profit,　ほとんど利益の無い

they decided / to change focus.　彼らは決めた / 目の向けどころを変えること

Ron says,　Ron は言う

"We thought of / how to monetize our plans.　私たちは〜を考えた / 私たちのプランを収益化する方法

Instead of just the booklets,　単なる小冊子の代わりに

we offered kits　私たちはキットを提供した

with all the parts　全ての部品と一緒に

needed to make the toys.　そのおもちゃを作るのに必要とされる

That was a turning point.　それが転機だった

Parents liked / the convenience of it,　親たちは好んだ / その便利さを

and the price was much lower　そして価格はかなり低かった

than store-bought toys."　店で買えるおもちゃよりも

And now,　そして今

two years / after that crucial decision,　2年 / その重要な決定の後

sales of Sci-kid kits are / around $200,000 per month.
Sci-kid のキットの売り上げは〜である / 月に約20万ドル

The company has plans / to expand their range　その会社には計画がある / 幅を広げるという

and begin overseas sales.　そして海外販売を始める

And Lucas still loves　そして Lucas はいまだに大好きだ

playing with his original toys!　彼のオリジナルのおもちゃで遊ぶこと

音読 トレーニング ③

Questions 5-7 refer to the following article. Track 03

A Company on the Up

Sci-kid Toys has been getting a lot of media attention lately for its imaginative science toys and kits. But success didn't come immediately for the company.

Founders Ron and Amanda Leyton, a married couple from Inverness, became disappointed when looking for stimulating toys for their 5-year-old son, Lucas. "There was nothing that required thought or skill", said Ron. So, three years ago, they started making toys with Lucas using their own ideas. Amanda explains, "We used household objects and wood to make moving cars, bottle rockets, and model cranes. Lucas loved it!"

Spotting a business opportunity, the pair started selling instructional booklets for their toys. However, the plans were soon copied and shared over the Internet. After a hard six months of little profit, they decided to change focus. Ron says, "We thought of how to monetize our plans. Instead of just the booklets, we offered kits with all the parts needed to make the toys. That was a turning point. Parents liked the convenience of it, and the price was much lower than store-bought toys."

And now, two years after that crucial decision, sales of Sci-kid kits are around $200,000 per month. The company has plans to expand their range and begin overseas sales. And Lucas still loves playing with his original toys!

Questions 8-11 / refer to / the following article.
問題 8-11 は / 〜に関するものです / 次の記事

February 10, Somersanville —　2月10日　Somersanville
Stanley Berg, / founder of E-Wave Burger,　Stanley Berg は / E-Wave Burger の創設者
has been named / the Small Business Owner of the Year　名前を挙げられた / 年間最優秀中小企業経営者
by the State Chamber of Commerce.　州の商工会議所によって
Gabe McCrane,　Gabe McCrane
vice president / of the Chamber,　副会長 / 商工会議所の
nominated Mr. Berg　Berg 氏を推薦した
for the award,　その賞に
basing his decision　彼の決定は基づいている
on the company's steady growth,　会社の着実な成長に
innovation, / and overall contribution　革新 / そして全体的な貢献
to the local community.　地域社会への
Those who know him　彼を知る人々は
believe that　〜ということを信じている
the main reason / for the company's success　主な理由 / 会社の成功の
is / the founder's enthusiasm / and longtime love
〜だ / 創設者の熱意 / そして長きにわたる愛情
for the restaurant business.　レストランビジネスに向けての

Mr. Berg was only twelve　Berg 氏はわずか12歳だった
when his parents opened / their family restaurant　彼の両親がオープンした時 / ファミリーレストランを
and he was instantly impressed / by it.　そして彼はすぐに強い印象を受けた / それによって
He cites / his mother's management skills　彼は挙げる / 彼の母の経営能力を
as his inspiration　彼の着想として
for getting involved in the industry.　この業界に関わることの

After graduating / from Waloo University in Chicago,　卒業した後 / Chicago の Waloo 大学を

he opened / two restaurants　彼はオープンした / 2 つのレストランを

with the financial backing　財政的な後ろ盾を伴って

of a local investor.　地元の投資家の

"Both locations were doing well,　両店舗とも順調だった

but / after the birth of my fourth child,　しかし / 4 人目の子供の誕生の後

running these restaurants / became overwhelming,"

これらのレストランを経営することが / 苦しくなってきた

Mr. Berg explained.　Berg 氏は説明した

"So, / I began thinking about　だから / 私は〜について考え始めた

how I could possibly use technology

どのように私はテクノロジーを使える可能性があるのか

to reduce / the need for labor　減らすために / 労働力の必要を

—including my own."　—私自身も含めて

He finally decided / to roll out / an entirely new line of dining places.

彼はついに決めた / 展開することを / 全く新しいタイプのレストランを

Partnering with Hania Ustad,　Hania Ustad と提携して

his college classmate / and owner of LA Botics Co.,

彼の大学のクラスメート / そして LA Botics 社のオーナー

he launched / the first　彼は始めた / 最初の一つを

of several partially automated delis.　いくつかの部分的に自動化されたデリの

These delis / specialize in / simple meals / such as hamburgers and sandwiches,

これらのデリは / 〜を専門としている / シンプルな食事 / ハンバーガーやサンドイッチのような

items / that are relatively simple　商品 / 比較的シンプルな

for robots to create.　ロボットが作るのに

The food is then carried / to the tables　食べ物はそれから届けられる / テーブルに

by conveyor belts / or robots on wheels.　ベルトコンベヤーによって / あるいは車輪の付いたロボットで

Best of all,　特に

since the delis have less than 30%　デリは 30 パーセントより少ないので
of competitors' staffing levels,　競合他社の人員レベルの
they are able to save money　彼らはお金を節約できる
and pass on the benefits / to customers　そして利益を渡す / 客に
in the form of lower prices.　低価格という形で

音読　トレーニング ④

Questions 8-11 refer to the following article.　🎧 Track 04

February 10, Somersanville —Stanley Berg, founder of E-Wave
Burger, has been named the Small Business Owner of the Year by
the State Chamber of Commerce. Gabe McCrane, vice president
of the Chamber, nominated Mr. Berg for the award, basing his
decision on the company's steady growth, innovation, and overall
contribution to the local community. Those who know him
believe that the main reason for the company's success is the
founder's enthusiasm and longtime love for the restaurant
business.

Mr. Berg was only twelve when his parents opened their family
restaurant and he was instantly impressed by it. He cites his
mother's management skills as his inspiration for getting
involved in the industry. After graduating from Waloo University
in Chicago, he opened two restaurants with the financial backing
of a local investor. "Both locations were doing well, but after the
birth of my fourth child, running these restaurants became
overwhelming," Mr. Berg explained. "So, I began thinking about
how I could possibly use technology to reduce the need for labor
—including my own."

He finally decided to roll out an entirely new line of dining places. Partnering with Hania Ustad, his college classmate and owner of LA Botics Co., he launched the first of several partially automated delis. These delis specialize in simple meals such as hamburgers and sandwiches, items that are relatively simple for robots to create. The food is then carried to the tables by conveyor belts or robots on wheels. Best of all, since the delis have less than 30% of competitors' staffing levels, they are able to save money and pass on the benefits to customers in the form of lower prices.

Questions 12-15 / refer to / the following online chat discussion.
問題 12-15 は / 〜に関するものです / 次のオンラインンチャットの話し合い

Gavin Page (10:13 A.M.)　Gavin Page（午前 10 時 13 分）
Hi everyone.　こんにちは、みなさん
I want to inform you　私はあなたたちに知らせたい
about some changes　いくつかの変更について
that will soon take place.　間もなく行われる

Vida Maras (10:14 A.M.)　Vida Maras（午前 10 時 14 分）
I've heard / some rumors.　私は聞きました / いくつかのうわさを
What are the specifics?　詳細は何ですか

Gavin Page (10:16 A.M.)　Gavin Page（午前 10 時 16 分）
We're going to be cutting / some of our operations staff
私たちは削減します / 何人かの運営スタッフを
in Minneapolis and London,　Minneapolis と London の
but increasing R&D staff　しかし研究開発スタッフを増やします
in Bangalore and Warsaw.　Bangalore と Warsaw の

Abdul Razak (10:17 A.M.)　Abdul Razak（午前 10 時 17 分）
What about my department?　私の部署はどうなりますか

Gavin Page (10:19 A.M.)　Gavin Page（午前 10 時 19 分）
Accounting will undergo / the biggest changes.　経理部は受けるでしょう / 最も大きな変更を
We're going to be outsourcing / nearly all　私たちは外注する予定です / ほぼ全てを
of those functions.　それらの機能の
We'll only keep you　私たちはあなただけを残します
and a small team / in our Boston headquarters.
そして小さなチームを / Boston 本社に

Abdul Razak (10:20 A.M.)　Abdul Razak（午前 10 時 20 分）

Well, / I did not see / this coming.　うーん / 分かりませんでした / こんなことに
なると

We posted / record profits / last year!　私たちは打ち立てました / 記録的な利益
を / 昨年

Gavin Page (10:22 A.M.)　Gavin Page（午前 10 時 22 分）

I know,　分かります

but the board thinks　しかし役員会は考えています

we need / to cut costs　私たちは必要がある / コストをカットする

to position us　私たちを配置する

for a stronger performance / next year.　もっと高い業績のために / 来年

Vikram Laghari (10:24 A.M.)　Vikram Laghari（午前 10 時 24 分）

When will this process start?　いつこのプロセスは始まりますか

It's already hard enough　それはすでに十分難しい

to find technical staff / here in Bangalore.　技術スタッフを見つけるのは / ここ
Bangalore で

Now, / you seem / to be giving me / new recruiting targets.
では / あなたは〜ように思える / 私に与えてくれる / 新しい採用目標を

Gavin Page (10:26 A.M.)　Gavin Page（午前 10 時 26 分）

This is all　これが全てです

I can tell you / at the moment.　私が話すことができるのは / 今のところ

Management will issue a memo　経営陣が連絡文書を出します

in a few days,　数日後に

and each department head will get / detailed instructions
そして各部門長は得るでしょう / 詳細な指示を

before our next big meeting.　次の大きな会議の前に

Questions 12-15 refer to the following online chat discussion. 🎧 Track 05

Gavin Page	**(10:13 A.M.)**

Hi everyone. I want to inform you about some changes that will soon take place.

Vida Maras   **(10:14 A.M.)**
I've heard some rumors. What are the specifics?

Gavin Page   **(10:16 A.M.)**
We're going to be cutting some of our operations staff in Minneapolis and London, but increasing R&D staff in Bangalore and Warsaw.

Abdul Razak   **(10:17 A.M.)**
What about my department?

Gavin Page   **(10:19 A.M.)**
Accounting will undergo the biggest changes. We're going to be outsourcing nearly all of those functions. We'll only keep you and a small team in our Boston headquarters.

Abdul Razak   **(10:20 A.M.)**
Well, I did not see this coming. We posted record profits last year!

Gavin Page   **(10:22 A.M.)**
I know, but the board thinks we need to cut costs to position us for a stronger performance next year.

Vikram Laghari   **(10:24 A.M.)**
When will this process start? It's already hard enough to find technical staff here in Bangalore. Now, you seem to be giving me new recruiting targets.

Gavin Page   **(10:26 A.M.)**
This is all I can tell you at the moment. Management will issue a memo in a few days, and each department head will get detailed instructions before our next big meeting.

スラッシュリーディング　トレーニング⑥

Questions 16-20 / refer to / the following Web site and e-mail.
問題 16-20 は / ～に関するものです / 次のウェブサイトと E メール

www.tomtombakery.com
Home ｜ Menu ｜ About Us ｜ News
ホーム　メニュー　当店について　ニュース

Posted / on 12 March　掲載された / 3 月 12 日に
Tom-Tom Bakery has been operating　Tom-Tom Bakery は営業している
in Gingham　Gingham で
for over fifteen years,　15 年以上の間
and we / have always tried / to give our customers / what they want.
そして私たちは / 常に～しようとしている / お客に与える / 彼らが欲しいものを
Therefore, / we are excited　したがって / 私たちはわくわくしている
about our newest project.　私たちの最新のプロジェクトについて
Besides serving / a wide range of delicious baked goods,
～を提供すること以外に / 様々な美味しい焼いた食品
we have decided / to begin holding baking classes
私たちは決めた / ベーキング教室を開催し始めることを
in the kitchen　キッチンで
of our main branch　私たちの本店の
near Gingham station.　Gingham 駅近くの
We hope / these classes will demonstrate the simplicity　私たちは願う / これらの教室が単純さを実証する
of the baking process.　ベーキングの工程の

Bread classes will be held　パン教室は開催される
on the first Wednesday / of each month,　第 1 水曜日に / 各月の
and cake classes / on the third Wednesday　そしてケーキ教室は / 第 3 水曜日に
(these are our regular closing days).　これらは当店の定休日だ
Lessons will begin / in April.　レッスンは始まる / 4 月に
Each session is limited / to fifteen participants,　各セッションは限られる / 15

人の参加者に

so / reservations are a must.　そのため / 予約が必須だ

You can book a spot　あなたは席を予約できる

by enquiring　問い合わせることによって

at any of our stores　私たちの店舗のいずれでも

in Gingham.　Gingham の

Please note that　〜にご注意ください

lessons are not / part of a continuous course.　レッスンは〜ではない / 連続したコースの一部

The same material will be taught / each time.　同じ教材が教えられる / 毎回

Questions 16-20 refer to the following Web site and e-mail. 🎧 Track 06

| ◀ ▶ | www.tomtombakery.com | | | C |

| Home | Menu | About Us | News |

Posted on 12 March

Tom-Tom Bakery has been operating in Gingham for over fifteen years, and we have always tried to give our customers what they want. Therefore, we are excited about our newest project. Besides serving a wide range of delicious baked goods, we have decided to begin holding baking classes in the kitchen of our main branch near Gingham station. We hope these classes will demonstrate the simplicity of the baking process.

Bread classes will be held on the first Wednesday of each month, and cake classes on the third Wednesday (these are our regular closing days). Lessons will begin in April. Each session is limited to fifteen participants, so reservations are a must. You can book a spot by enquiring at any of our stores in Gingham.

Please note that lessons are not part of a continuous course. The same material will be taught each time.

To: ellis.f@towncitymail.com　宛先：ellis.f@towncitymail.com
From: classes@tomtombakery.com　送信者：classes@tomtombakery.com
Date: 22 April　日付：4月22日
Subject: Class confirmation　件名：教室の確認

よりぬき！テスト

解説

攻略法

トレーニング

確認テスト

解説

トレーニング

Hello Ms. Ellis, こんにちは、Ellis さん

I am writing 私は書いている
to confirm your place あなたの席を確認するため
in the May baking class. ５月のベーキング教室の
You will be making / strawberry shortcake! あなたは作ります / いちごのショートケーキを
As you paid the fee あなたは費用を支払ったので
when you made your reservation あなたが予約をしたときに
in the store, 店で
all you need to do is / bring a clean apron
あなたがする必要のある全ては / 清潔なエプロンを持ってくる
and wear something そしてなにかを身に着ける
you don't mind / getting slightly dirty. あなたが気にならない / 少し汚れること

Because the classes are held / on days 教室は行われるので / 日々に
when the bakery is closed, ベーカリーが閉まっているとき
you will need to use / the rear entrance. あなたは使う必要がある / 裏口を
You can reach it あなたはそれに着くことができる
by walking 歩くことによって
along Miller Street. Miller Street に沿って

I look forward to / seeing you / in class. 私は〜を楽しみにしている / あなたに
会うこと / 教室で

Sincerely, よろしくお願いします

Raymond LeClair, Raymond LeClair
Assistant Head Baker パン製造長補佐
Tom-Tom Bakery Tom-Tom Bakery

音読 トレーニング ⑦

🎧 Track 07

To:	<ellis.f@towncitymail.com>
From:	<classes@tomtombakery.com>
Date:	22 April
Subject:	Class confirmation

Hello Ms. Ellis,

I am writing to confirm your place in the May baking class. You will be making strawberry shortcake! As you paid the fee when you made your reservation in the store, all you need to do is bring a clean apron and wear something you don't mind getting slightly dirty.

Because the classes are held on days when the bakery is closed, you will need to use the rear entrance. You can reach it by walking along Miller Street.

I look forward to seeing you in class.

Sincerely,

Raymond LeClair, Assistant Head Baker
Tom-Tom Bakery

スラッシュリーディング トレーニング ⑧

Questions 21-25 / refer to / the following Web page, letter, and article.
問題 21-25 は / ～に関するものです / 次のウェブページ、手紙、そして記事

www.dalehill-town.org.uk/recreation/news
Posted / 05 May　掲載された / 5月5日
Notice of Development / at Highmoor Park　開発のお知らせ / Highmoor 公園での

The Parks and Recreation department　公園緑地部
of Dalehill's town council　Dalehill 町議会の
has approved the construction　建設を承認した
of an all-weather rock-climbing facility　全天候型のロッククライミング施設の
at Highmoor Park.　Highmoor 公園での
The proposals were submitted　提案は提出された
by unpaid community youth leaders　無給の地域の若者のリーダーたちによって
wishing to provide / more amenities　提供することを願って / よりたくさんの公共施設を
for the young people　若者たちのために
of Dalehill.　Dalehill の
It will be built　それは建てられる
on an unused grassy area　使われていない草地の上に
bordering Jacob Street.　Jacob Street に隣接している

Construction will begin / on July 10,　建設は始まる / 7 月 10 日に
and the climbing wall is expected　そしてクライミング用の壁は期待されている
to be open to the public / at the end of September.　一般へのオープンを / 9 月末に
The final cost / has yet to be confirmed　最終的な費用は / まだ確認されていない
but will appear / on this Web site　しかし現れるだろう / このウェブサイトに
in the coming days.　数日後に

The council hopes / to keep the rock-climbing area　議会は望む / ロッククライミングエリアを保つことを
free of any entry fees,　いかなる入場料もかからない
but it reserves the right / to introduce charges　しかしそれは権利を有する / 有料にすること
if running costs are higher / than expected.　もし運営費が高かったら / 予想よりも

トレーニング ⑧

Questions **21-25** refer to the following Web page, letter, and article.

🎧 Track 08

www.dalehill-town.org.uk/recreation/news

Posted 05 May

Notice of Development at Highmoor Park

The Parks and Recreation department of Dalehill's town council has approved the construction of an all-weather rock-climbing facility at Highmoor Park. The proposals were submitted by unpaid community youth leaders wishing to provide more amenities for the young people of Dalehill. It will be built on an unused grassy area bordering Jacob Street.

Construction will begin on July 10, and the climbing wall is expected to be open to the public at the end of September. The final cost has yet to be confirmed but will appear on this Web site in the coming days.

The council hopes to keep the rock-climbing area free of any entry fees, but it reserves the right to introduce charges if running costs are higher than expected.

スラッシュリーディング　トレーニング ⑨

May 22　5月22日
Parks and Recreation Dept.　公園緑地部
Dalehill Town Council　Dalehill 町議会
21-39 High Road　21-39 High Road
Dalehill DH5 8UI　Dalehill DH5 8UI

よりぬき！テスト

解説

攻略法

トレーニング

確認テスト

解説

トレーニング

To whom it may concern:　ご担当者様

I am writing / regarding the plans　私は書いている / 計画に関して
for a rock-climbing area / in Highmoor Park,　ロッククライミングエリアの / Highmoor 公園にある
which I learned of / on the council Web site.　そのことを私は知った / 議会のウェブサイトで
While I recognize the need　私が必要性を認識している一方で
to provide more things to do　より多くのすべきことを提供する
for the young people / of Dalehill,　若者たちに / Dalehill の
I believe　私は思う
the proposed site should be reconsidered.　提案された用地は考え直されるべきだ
Far from being an "unused grassy area",　未使用の草地からは程遠い
that part of the park is very popular　公園のその部分は非常に人気がある
with dog walkers / like me.　犬の散歩をする人たちに / 私のような
The benches there are frequently used　そこにあるベンチは頻繁に使用される
for resting / and for eating lunch.　休憩するために / そして昼食を食べるために
I know this　私はこれを知っている
as my house is / directly opposite the area.　私の家が〜なので / そのエリアの真向かい

I am sure　私は確信している
an alternative location can be found　代替となる場所が見つけられる
before construction begins.　建設が始まる前に

Regards,　よろしくお願いします

Michael Newton　Michael Newton

Track 09

May 22

Parks and Recreation Dept.
Dalehill Town Council
21-39 High Road
Dalehill DH5 8UI

To whom it may concern:

I am writing regarding the plans for a rock-climbing area in Highmoor Park, which I learned of on the council Web site. While I recognize the need to provide more things to do for the young people of Dalehill, I believe the proposed site should be reconsidered. Far from being an "unused grassy area", that part of the park is very popular with dog walkers like me. The benches there are frequently used for resting and for eating lunch. I know this as my house is directly opposite the area.

I am sure an alternative location can be found before construction begins.

Regards,

Michael Newton

よりぬき！テスト

解説

攻略法

トレーニング

確認テスト

解説

トレーニング

Young Citizens / Delighted With New Facility　若い市民たち / 新しい施設に喜ぶ

(October 24) ―　10月24日

Highmoor Park was buzzing　Highmoor公園はにぎわっていた

with excitement / yesterday　興奮で / 昨日

as the mayor formally opened / a new rock-climbing area.
市長が正式にオープンしたので / 新しいロッククライミングエリアを

The outdoor facility consists of a four-meter high
そのアウトドア施設は4メートルの高さから成る

and 35-meter long wall　そして35メートルの長さの壁

with various hand grips / to grab onto.　様々なハンドグリップがある / つかむための

On its first day,　初日には

over one hundred people enjoyed / testing their skills.
100人以上の人たちが楽しんだ / 自身のスキルを試すこと

While most were youngsters,　多くが若者である一方で

there were quite a few adults　かなりの数の大人たちがいた

having a go, / too.　やってみる / 同じように

Community youth worker Annabel Brines　地域の若い労働者であるAnnabel Brinesは

couldn't be happier,　これ以上ないくらい幸せだ

saying,　言う

"This is a great way / to get　これは素晴らしい方法だ / ~させる

not only young people, / but all citizens　若者だけでなく / 全ての市民に

to exercise / and enjoy the outdoors."　運動する / そしてアウトドアを楽しむ

音読 トレーニング ⑩

🎧 Track 10

Young Citizens Delighted With New Facility

(October 24)—Highmoor Park was buzzing with excitement yesterday as the mayor formally opened a new rock-climbing area. The outdoor facility consists of a four-meter high and 35-meter long wall with various hand grips to grab onto. On its first day, over one hundred people enjoyed testing their skills. While most were youngsters, there were quite a few adults having a go, too.

Community youth worker Annabel Brines couldn't be happier, saying, "This is a great way to get not only young people, but all citizens to exercise and enjoy the outdoors."

よりぬき！テスト

解説

攻略法

トレーニング

確認テスト

解説

トレーニング

5 | トレーニング 設問をストックする

　ここまで、Part7 の問題文を活用してトレーニングしてきましたが、実際に解く際は設問も速く理解できると解答スピードがいっそう上がります。

　p.94-96 でご紹介した、Part7 に登場する主な設問タイプについても、読んですぐ理解できるようにトレーニングしておきましょう。一瞬で理解できる設問のストックを増やしておくことで、テストを解く際にリテンションの負担が減り、時間的にも気持ち的にも余裕が生まれてきます。

スラッシュリーディング　トレーニング ①

① ピンポイント情報について問う設問

1. What / is suggested / about the invoice?　何 / 示唆されている / 請求書について

2. What / is Ms. Hayasaka / asked / to do?　何 / ハヤサカさん / 求められる / すること

3. When / will the discount / be applied / to the merchandise?　いつ / 割引は / 適用される / 商品に

4. Where / does Mr. Naito / work?　どこで / ナイトウさんは / 働く

5. Who / most likely / is Hiromu?　誰 / おそらく / ヒロムは

6. Who / will be surveyed?　誰 / 調査される

7. What / is true / about Mr. Sanada?　何 / 正しい / サナダさんについて

8. According to the notice, / what / will occur / this weekend?　お知らせによれば / 何 / 起こる / 今週末

9. At what time / will the flower shop / open / during the summer?　何時に /
花屋は / 開店する / 夏の間

10. What / is available / in the London location?　何 / 入手できる / ロンドンの
店舗で

11. What / is offered / to those who purchased / an electric chain saw?
何 / 与えられる / 〜を買った人に / 電動のこぎり

12. When / will the interview / take place?　いつ / 面接は / 行われる

13. When / is the deadline / for the report / to be submitted?　いつ / 期限は /
レポートの / 提出される

14. How often / should the light bulbs / be replaced?　どのくらいの頻度 / 電
球は〜べきか / 交換される

15. For how long / has Mr. Watanabe stayed / in the U.S.?　どのくらいの間 /
ワタナベさんは滞在してるか / アメリカに

16. Where / will the conference / be held?　どこで / 会議は / 開催される

音読 トレーニング ①

① ピンポイント情報について問う設問　　　　　　　　 Track 11

1. What is suggested about the invoice?
2. What is Ms. Hayasaka asked to do?
3. When will the discount be applied to the merchandise?
4. Where does Mr. Naito work?
5. Who most likely is Hiromu?
6. Who will be surveyed?
7. What is true about Mr. Sanada?

よりぬき！テスト

解説

攻略法

トレーニング

確認テスト

解説

トレーニング

8. According to the notice, what will occur this weekend?

9. At what time will the flower shop open during the summer?

10. What is available in the London location?

11. What is offered to those who purchased an electric chain saw?

12. When will the interview take place?

13. When is the deadline for the report to be submitted?

14. How often should the light bulbs be replaced?

15. For how long has Mr. Watanabe stayed in the U.S.?

16. Where will the conference be held?

スラッシュリーディング トレーニング ②

② 問題文全体について問う設問

1. What / is the purpose / of the letter?　何 / 目的は / 手紙の

2. What / is the subject / of the memo?　何 / 主題は / メモの

3. Why / was the e-mail / written?　なぜ / Eメールは / 書かれた

4. What / does the Web page / explain?　何 / ウェブページは / 説明する

5. What type of business / is LIJ co.?　何のタイプの会社 / LIJ 社は

6. For whom / is this memo / most likely / intended?　誰に / このメモは / おそらく / 向けられる

7. What / will be discussed / at the today's meeting?　何 / 話し合われる / 今日の会議で

8. What product / will be reviewed?　何の商品 / レビューされる

9. Where / would the article / most likely / appear?　どこに / 記事は / おそらく / 載る

142

10. What / is being described / on the Web site?　何 / 書かれている / ウェブサイトに

11. What / is being advertised?　何 / 宣伝されている

12. Where / would the notice / most likely / appear?　どこに / お知らせは / おそらく / 載る

音読　トレーニング ②

② 問題文全体について問う設問　 Track 12

1. What is the purpose of the letter?
2. What is the subject of the memo?
3. Why was the e-mail written?
4. What does the Web page explain?
5. What type of business is LIJ co.?
6. For whom is this memo most likely intended?
7. What will be discussed at the today's meeting?
8. What product will be reviewed?
9. Where would the article most likely appear?
10. What is being described on the Web site?
11. What is being advertised?
12. Where would the notice most likely appear?

スラッシュリーディング　トレーニング ③

③ NOT 問題

1. What / does Mr. Okada / NOT offer / to provide?　何 / オカダさんが / 申し出ていない / 提供すると

2. What / is NOT stated / about the Big Peach Airlines?　何 / 述べられていな

よりぬき！テスト

解説

攻略法

トレーニング

確認テスト

解説

トレーニング

い / Big Peach Airlines について

3. What / is NOT advertised / in today's newspaper?　何 / 宣伝されていない / 今日の新聞で

4. What / is NOT enclosed / in the letter?　何 / 同封されていない / 手紙に

音読 トレーニング ③

③ NOT 問題

 Track 13

1. What does Mr. Okada NOT offer to provide?
2. What is NOT stated about the Big Peach Airlines?
3. What is NOT advertised in today's newspaper?
4. What is NOT enclosed in the letter?

Chapter

3

確認テスト
問題

Tekkin X: The latest soccer boots from the footwear specialist, Varhaven Outdoors.

Tekkin X boots are the ultimate choice for comfort and durability for the serious player.

- Special coating keeps feet dry even in the wettest conditions
- Hand-stitched in Germany by our craftspeople
- Available in electric yellow and classic navy

As with all our boots, they come in a range of sizes to fit narrow and wide feet. Get yours today from your local sporting goods store - competitively priced at $95.00. You can find further information on Tekkin X, together with our range of sneakers and ski boots, by visiting www.varhavenoutdoors. org.

1. What is NOT an advertised feature of the boots?

    (A) They have color options.
    (B) They are made by hand.
    (C) They are lightweight.
    (D) They are waterproof.

2. What is indicated about Varhaven Outdoors?

    (A) It manufactures in multiple countries.
    (B) It offers regular discounts.
    (C) Its products can be purchased online.
    (D) It makes a variety of footwear.

よりぬき！テスト

解説

攻略法

トレーニング

確認テスト

解説

トレーニング

Questions 3-4 refer to the following notice.

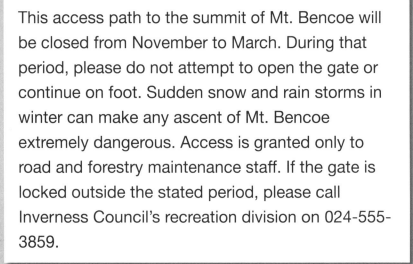

ATTENTION

This access path to the summit of Mt. Bencoe will be closed from November to March. During that period, please do not attempt to open the gate or continue on foot. Sudden snow and rain storms in winter can make any ascent of Mt. Bencoe extremely dangerous. Access is granted only to road and forestry maintenance staff. If the gate is locked outside the stated period, please call Inverness Council's recreation division on 024-555-3859.

3. For whom is the notice intended?

(A) Mountain climbers
(B) Maintenance workers
(C) Local farmers
(D) Truck drivers

4. Why does the path sometimes close?

(A) Regular repairs are necessary.
(B) Weather conditions are often treacherous.
(C) There is a lack of qualified safety personnel.
(D) The surrounding nature needs to be protected.

Arusa Café

Quality Coffee, Great Times

To celebrate the March reopening of our Fifth Street, Fakeham branch, please use this beverage coupon anytime until the end of May. The coupon can be used on any standard menu item, excluding fresh juices and frozen yogurts.

This coupon can only be used with orders exceeding $10.00. There is a limit of one free beverage per coupon. Further copies can be made by visiting our Web site. This promotion applies only to the Fifth Street, Fakeham outlet of Arusa Café.

www.arusa-cafe.co.uk

5. For what can the coupon be used?

(A) An orange juice
(B) A dessert
(C) A soda
(D) A sandwich

6. What is NOT true about the coupon offer?

(A) It can be used in April.
(B) Users must purchase other items.
(C) More than one person can use it.
(D) Additional coupons can be printed at home.

7. What is implied about Arusa Café?

(A) It operates in multiple locations.
(B) It opened five years ago.
(C) It serves freshly-made food.
(D) It offers the coupon annually.

What's Happening in Corkstone

CORKSTONE (July 10)— Residents going to Corkstone train station may want to rethink how they get there. In line with the city's stated goal of reducing carbon emissions from local travel, a new building for parking bicycles has opened beside the station. — [1] —.

City officials hope the free-to-use facility will encourage more citizens to cycle to the station. The building features secure parking, and the enclosed space protects bicycles from the weather. The running costs will be partly funded by increased car parking charges around the station area. — [2] —. Although there is no charge, passes are needed to use the bicycle parking. This allows City Hall to monitor user numbers. People can get one directly from the office at the facility's entrance. — [3] —.

Bicycle shop owner Liam Kane welcomed the policy. "It's a fantastic way to promote cycling. Bicycles are great for the earth and for your health." — [4] —. Mayor Harrison commented, "We're seeing more and more families choosing to live in Corkstone, which is wonderful, but it must not lead to increased traffic on our roads. Journeys made by bicycle have a part to play in keeping cars off the road."

8. What does the article discuss?

(A) A city's environmental policy
(B) The launch of a public transport network
(C) New ways to attract families to a city
(D) Improvements to a train station building

9. Where can passes be obtained?

(A) At City Hall
(B) In local bicycle shops
(C) In the station ticket office
(D) Next to the station

10. What did Mayor Harrison imply about Corkstone?

(A) It needs to attract investments.
(B) Citizens are not happy with travel charges.
(C) Its population is rising.
(D) Car drivers should be more careful.

11. In which of the positions marked [1], [2], [3], and [4] does the following sentence best belong?

"It is hoped that the fees will further push people to change their habits."

(A) [1]
(B) [2]
(C) [3]
(D) [4]

Questions 12-15 refer to the following online chat discussion.

Michelle Groves [10:20 A.M.]: Good morning Anna and Pascal. Most of the details of your catering order have been finalized. I'll be making the necessary purchases today and tomorrow. I just need to confirm whether there are any dietary needs or not.

Anna Nakamura [10:22 A.M.]: Hi Michelle. What do you mean exactly?

Michelle Groves [10:23 A.M.]: For example, some people may be allergic to nuts or perhaps some do not eat meat.

Anna Nakamura [10:25 A.M.]: I get you. Pascal will know that better than me. Pascal?

Pascal Levant [10:28 A.M.]: No one has mentioned anything to me.

Michelle Groves [10:30 A.M.]: OK. I'm planning to top the cake with nuts, so I'll go ahead with that. And there will some basic vegetarian dishes anyway.

Anna Nakamura [10:31 A.M.]: Good to know. What time can we expect you to arrive on the 23rd?

Michelle Groves [10:33 A.M.]: Around 11. That reminds me – will it be possible to leave my van near the main entrance? I have a lot of things to unload, and I'd rather not carry them too far.

Anna Nakamura [10:36 A.M.]: Leave it to me. I'll make sure there's a space for you.

Pascal Levant [10:38 A.M.]: And I'll be there to greet you when you arrive. Everything needs to be perfect for our German colleagues. We want them to experience some genuine American hospitality!

12. What does Ms. Groves want to confirm?

(A) The size of the order
(B) The final cost of the event
(C) The type of ingredients
(D) The number of attendees

13. At 10:28 A.M., what does Mr. Levant most likely mean when he writes, "No one has mentioned anything to me"?

(A) Special options are not required.
(B) Ms. Groves should wait for a response.
(C) He is surprised at a menu item.
(D) His previous cost estimate was correct.

14. What is Ms. Groves concerned about?

(A) She may not have enough food containers.
(B) She may require help to unload her vehicle.
(C) She may not have enough time to set up.
(D) She may need to park some distance from the venue.

15. Why most likely is the event being held?

(A) A manager is going to retire.
(B) Overseas staff will visit the company.
(C) A new product will be launched.
(D) A European branch office will open.

Questions 16-20 refer to the following article and e-mail.

19 April — Vue Garden Hotel Group will open another hotel in Pattaya later this year, which will bring much-needed jobs to the area. The hotel will have 150 rooms along with formal meeting facilities, as Vue Garden hopes to attract business travelers as well as traditional vacationers. Unlike the group's existing hotel in the town, this one will feature exclusive access to a 100-meter stretch of beach to enjoy swimming in the bay's crystal clear waters. Plans also show an upscale dining option, a gym and sauna, and an event hall.

People wishing to apply for a position at the hotel, which will open in October, should visit the group's Web site and complete the job application form. According to a Vue Garden statement, people with experience in customer service or room cleaning are especially needed. However, the group is looking to hire young people with no previous work experience as part of their kitchen crew in order to train them in Vue Garden's unique cooking methods. The application deadline is July 1, with training for new employees beginning one month later.

To:	Ally Thongsuk <happyally@usendmail.com>
From:	Henri Poll <poll.h@vuegardenhotel.com>
Date:	5 July
Subject:	Job application
Attachment:	Information

Dear Ms. Thongsuk,

Thank you for completing an online application for our new hotel in Pattaya. After careful consideration, we would like you to attend an interview to discuss your desire to join us as a junior kitchen assistant. Interviews will be held at Quantum Business Park on 14 July. Please see the attached information for directions and times. There is a frequent public bus service to the park.

We expect all applicants to arrive on time and to be formally dressed. As the interview will take place over two sessions, a complimentary lunch will be provided. As preparation for the interview, we hope you can research Vue Garden's mission statement and history. These can be found on our Web site.

Warmest regards,

Henri Poll
Assistant Manager

16. What is true of Vue Garden's new hotel?

(A) It will be built on the site of an existing hotel.
(B) It will be the group's second branch in Pattaya.
(C) It will focus on luxury guest rooms.
(D) It will likely open ahead of schedule.

17. What will NOT be a facility of the hotel?

(A) A private beach
(B) A fitness center
(C) A swimming pool
(D) Conference rooms

18. What will happen in August?

(A) Staff will receive training.
(B) Interviews will be held.
(C) The hotel will accept bookings.
(D) A promotional event will take place.

19. What is implied about Ms. Thongsuk?

(A) She already met Mr. Poll.
(B) She will deal with hotel guests.
(C) She was late in sending her application.
(D) She has never worked in a hotel.

20. What will be provided at Quantum Business Park?

(A) Complimentary transportation
(B) An information packet
(C) A free meal
(D) Staff uniforms

Questions 21-25 refer to the following e-mail, brochure, and notice.

From:	human.resources@tvb-insurance.com
To:	dewan.v@tvb-insurance.com
Date:	9 September
Subject:	Reach Out courses

Dear Vikram Dewan,

We at Human Resources received notification through your section head, Paula Ingram, of your interest in completing a course at our training partner, Reach Out Education. We will be delighted to support you in your wish to improve and update your first aid skills. This will benefit not only you, but those around you if there is ever an accident or injury in the office. After finishing the course, we may ask you to run an informal workshop for your colleagues to pass on your skills.

The course will be held at Reach Out's office in central Leeds on every Tuesday in October and November. Needless to say, you will be given paid time off to attend the course, and all fees will be covered by TVB Insurance.

I will forward you further information as I receive it from Reach Out.

Sally Milligan
Head of Human Resources

Reach Out Education
32-35 Hanover St.
Leeds LS2 9OL
Tel: (0133) 555-4040

Reach Out Education's classroom-based courses cover a wide variety of topics aimed at those in work, in education, or searching for employment. Passing one of our programs means you'll leave with a nationally-recognized qualification to boost your career prospects. With maximum class sizes of fifteen people, each student has plenty of time with both their lead course instructor and assistant teacher.

October-November Class Offerings on Workplace Safety

Hygiene
For food preparation staff. Learn the essentials of safe food handling techniques and cleanliness in order to prevent sickness and to comply with national laws.

Fire Safety
This class covers what to do in a fire emergency. Learn how to act, how to direct colleagues to safety, and basic survival skills. You'll also learn fire prevention strategies.

Working Smart
Study techniques on avoiding common workplace injuries that often happen when lifting heavy items or not using the correct equipment. This can lead to a CityTec qualification in workplace safety.

Quick Response
Learn how to deal with a variety of medical emergencies before the professionals arrive. Your quick actions could save the life of a colleague. The course covers basic biology, covering wounds, and treating shock.

NOTICE

The policy on payments for textbooks has changed. Course fees will no longer include the cost of course materials. Please pay for your textbooks on the day of your first class by going to the student affairs office on the first floor. Remember to bring your student identification number. This does not apply to those whose fees are being paid by their employer. In such cases, kindly collect an invoice from student affairs and give it to the relevant person in your workplace. Students repeating courses should check with their lead instructor to confirm that the course materials are unchanged.

21. Why was the e-mail sent?

(A) To ask for proof of qualifications

(B) To give advice on scheduling a course

(C) To request help running a workshop

(D) To approve a request for training

22. What is indicated about courses at Reach Out Education?

(A) Each is conducted by two teaching staff members.

(B) Some are free of charge for unemployed people.

(C) They feature some online lessons.

(D) They take place in multiple locations.

23. What course will Mr. Dewan take?

(A) Hygiene

(B) Fire Safety

(C) Working Smart

(D) Quick Response

24. What does Mr. Dewan need to do regarding his course books?

(A) Pass a bill to his employer

(B) Buy course materials from a bookstore

(C) Pay at the student affairs office

(D) Talk to his course instructor

25. In the notice, the phrase "apply to" in paragraph 1, line 6, is closest in meaning to

(A) request

(B) concern

(C) administer

(D) repair

確認テスト　解答一覧

Part 7	正答
1	C
2	D
3	A
4	B
5	C
6	C
7	A
8	A
9	D
10	C
11	B
12	C
13	A
14	D
15	B
16	B
17	C
18	A
19	D
20	C
21	D
22	A
23	D
24	A
25	B

確認テスト
解説

Tekkin X: The latest soccer boots from the footwear specialist, Varhaven Outdoors.

Tekkin X boots are the ultimate choice for comfort and durability for the serious player.

- ❶Special coating keeps feet dry even in the wettest conditions
- ❷Hand-stitched in Germany by our craftspeople
- ❸Available in electric yellow and classic navy

As with all our boots, they come in a range of sizes to fit narrow and wide feet. Get yours today from your local sporting goods store - competitively priced at $95.00. ❹You can find further information on Tekkin X, together with our range of sneakers and ski boots, by visiting www.varhavenoutdoors.org.

問題 1-2 は次の広告に関するものです。

Tekkin X: 靴のスペシャリスト、Varhaven Outdoors の最新サッカーシューズ

Tekkin X シューズは快適性と耐久性を追求する本気のアスリートにとって最高の選択です。

・特別なコーティングにより、非常に水分のある状況でも足を乾いた状態に保ちます
・ドイツで職人によって手縫いされています
・蛍光イエローとクラシックネイビーがございます

当社のどの靴とも同様に、足幅の狭い方にも広い方にも合うサイズ展開です。お近くのスポーツ用品店で今すぐお買い求めください ― 他社と比べてお求めやすい 95 ドルです。Tekkin X の詳細は、当社のスニーカーやスキー靴も合わせて www.varhavenoutdoors.org にアクセスすることでご確認いただけます。

語句

□ latest 最新の　□ boot ブーツ、靴　□ footwear 靴　□ specialist 専門家
□ ultimate 究極の、最高の　□ choice 選択　□ comfort 快適さ
□ durability 丈夫さ　□ serious 本気の　□ coating コーティング
□ feet 足（foot の複数形）　□ even 〜でさえ　□ wet 濡れている
□ condition 状態　□ hand-stitched 手縫いをされた　□ Germany ドイツ
□ craftspeople 職人　□ available 入手できる　□ electric 派手な、鮮やかな
□ as with 〜と同様に　□ come in 〜の形で売られる　□ a range of 様々な〜
□ fit 〜にフィットする　□ narrow 狭い　□ wide 幅広い　□ local 地元の
□ sporting goods store スポーツ用品店　□ competitively 競争的に
□ priced at 〜という価格で　□ further information 詳しい情報
□ together with 〜と一緒に　□ range of 〜の範囲
□ by doing 〜することによって

1. What is NOT an advertised feature of the boots?

(A) They have color options.
(B) They are made by hand.
(C) They are lightweight.
(D) They are waterproof.

この靴の特徴として広告されていないのはどれですか。

(A) 色の選択肢がある。
(B) 手作業で作られている。
(C) 軽量である。
(D) 耐水性がある。

正解 C

解説

NOT問題は本文の内容に合致する3つを選び、残った1つを正解とします。
(A) は箇条書きの❸ Available in electric yellow and classic navy「蛍光イエローとクラシックネイビーがございます」に、(B) は❷ Hand-stitched in Germany by our craftspeople「ドイツで職人によって手縫いされています」に、(D) は❶ Special coating keeps feet dry even in the wettest conditions「特別なコーティングにより、非常に水分のある状況でも足を乾いた状態に保ちます」に述べられています。よって、正解は (C) です。

❶本文→選択肢の言い換え

(A) Available in electric yellow and classic navy
➡ have color options
(B) Hand-stitched ➡ made by hand
(D) keeps feet dry even in the wettest conditions ➡ waterproof

語句
□ advertise 〜を宣伝する　□ feature 特徴　□ option 選択肢
□ by hand 手作業で　□ lightweight 軽い
□ waterproof 防水加工をした、耐水の

166

One-up NOT 問題の解答方法

設問に NOT がある問題を、本書では NOT 問題と呼んでいます。NOT 問題を効率よく解くためには、以下の手順で解答することをお勧めします。

NOT 問題の解答手順

① （A）～（D）の選択肢に目を通す

その際、できる限り選択肢の内容を頭に叩き込み、記憶するつもりで読むようにします。

②問題文を読み進め、選択肢の内容と一致するものを 3 つ見つける

③問題文の内容と一致せずに残ったものを正解としてマークする

2. What is indicated about Varhaven Outdoors?

(A) It manufactures in multiple countries.

(B) It offers regular discounts.

(C) Its products can be purchased online.

(D) It makes a variety of footwear.

Varhaven Outdoors について何が示されていますか。

(A) 複数の国で生産している。

(B) 定期的な割引を提供している。

(C) 製品はオンラインで購入可能である。

(D) 様々な靴を作っている。

正解 **D**

解説

問題文後半の❹に You can find further information on Tekkin X, together with our range of sneakers and ski boots, by visiting www.varhavenoutdoors. org.「Tekkin X の詳細は、当社のスニーカーやスキー靴も合わせて www. varhavenoutdoors.org にアクセスすることでご確認いただけます」とあります。Varhaven Outdoors は様々な種類の靴を製造していることが分かるため、正解は（D）です。

our range of sneakers and ski boots
➡ a variety of footwear

語句

☐ manufacture 〜を製造する　☐ multiple 複数の　☐ offer 〜を提供する
☐ regular 定期的な　☐ discount 割引　☐ product 製品
☐ purchase 〜を購入する　☐ online オンラインで　☐ a variety of 様々な〜

みんなのお悩み＆おすすめの解答方法 ②

悩み

「数行読んでも問題文の概要がつかめません、どうしたらいいでしょうか？」

解答

　文書を読んで概要を把握するトレーニングをやってみてください。

　Part 7 のシングルパッセージのうち、比較的短めの問題文を読み、1 文 1 文をきちんと理解できるかどうか判断します。

　英文を読めない、理解できない理由は、語彙力の足りなさと文法力の足りなさに起因します。

　知らない単語は意味と品詞、発音をきちんと確認してください。

　また、全ての単語が分かるのに文が読めない場合には、その文における何らかの文法事項が理解できていないことがほとんどです。

　その問題集や参考書の解説をよく読んで理解し、知らない文法事項（例えば分詞構文や仮定法などのような文法項目）がある場合には、高校生が使うような英文法の本を 1 冊用意して、それを参考にして英文を理解してみてください。

TOEIC L&R テスト対策の学習にお薦めの英文法書
『総合英語 FACTBOOK これからの英文法』
大西泰斗、ポール・マクベイ（著）
桐原書店

Questions 3-4 refer to the following notice.

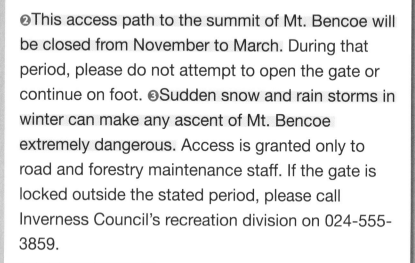

ATTENTION

②This access path to the summit of Mt. Bencoe will be closed from November to March. During that period, please do not attempt to open the gate or continue on foot. ③Sudden snow and rain storms in winter can make any ascent of Mt. Bencoe extremely dangerous. Access is granted only to road and forestry maintenance staff. If the gate is locked outside the stated period, please call Inverness Council's recreation division on 024-555-3859.

問題 3-4 は次のお知らせに関するものです。

注意

Bencoe 山の頂上へのこの山道は 11 月から 3 月まで閉鎖します。この期間、この門を開けたり歩いてこの先を進んだりしようとしないでください。冬場の急な吹雪や暴風雨で Bencoe 山へ登るのが極めて危険になる恐れがあります。道路や森林地の保守担当者に限りアクセスが認められます。上記期間外で門が施錠されている場合は、Inverness 地方議会のレクリエーション課、024-555-3859 まで電話してください。

【語句】

- [ ] attention 注意 　[ ] access 経路、アクセス　[ ] path 小道
- [ ] summit 頂上　[ ] from A to B AからBまで　[ ] during ～の間
- [ ] period 期間　[ ] attempt to do ～しようと試みる　[ ] gate 門
- [ ] continue 進み続ける　[ ] on foot 徒歩で　[ ] sudden 突然の
- [ ] rain storm 暴風雨　[ ] make A B AをBにする　[ ] ascent 登ること
- [ ] extremely 極端に　[ ] dangerous 危険な　[ ] grant ～を認める
- [ ] forestry 森林地　[ ] maintenance staff 保守担当者
- [ ] lock ～に鍵を掛ける　[ ] outside ～以外で　[ ] stated 表明された
- [ ] council 地方議会　[ ] division 部門、課

3. For whom is the notice intended?

(A) Mountain climbers
(B) Maintenance workers
(C) Local farmers
(D) Truck drivers

このお知らせは誰に向けられていますか。

(A) 登山者
(B) 保守作業員
(C) 地元の農家
(D) トラック運転手

正解　A

解説

タイトルに❶ ATTENTION「注意」とあり、問題文の冒頭に❷ This access path to the summit of Mt. Bencoe will be closed from November to March.「Bencoe 山の頂上へのこの山道は 11 月から 3 月まで閉鎖します」とあります。この注意書きは登山道にあることが分かるため、正解は（A）です。

❶本文→選択肢の言い換え

ATTENTION, This access path to the summit of Mt. Bencoe
➡ the notice intended for, Mountain climbers

語句
□ be intended for 〜を対象としている　□ climber 登る人　□ local 地元の
□ farmer 農家

4. Why does the path sometimes close?

(A) Regular repairs are necessary.
(B) Weather conditions are often treacherous.
(C) There is a lack of qualified safety personnel.
(D) The surrounding nature needs to be protected.

この山道が時々閉鎖するのはなぜですか。

(A) 定期的な修繕が必要である。
(B) 天気状況が不安定になりやすい。
(C) 資格のある安全対策担当者が不足している。
(D) 周囲の自然は守られる必要がある。

正解 **B**

解説

❸ に Sudden snow and rain storms in winter can make any ascent of Mt. Bencoe extremely dangerous.「冬場の急な吹雪や暴風雨で Bencoe 山へ登るのが極めて危険になる恐れがあります」と述べられています。これを treacherous「不安定だ」を使った言い換えで天候状態を表している (B) が正解となります。

語句

□ regular 定期的な　□ repair 修繕　□ necessary 必要だ
□ weather condition 天候　□ treacherous 不安定だ　□ lack 不足
□ qualified 資格のある　□ personnel 職員　□ surrounding 周囲の
□ nature 自然　□ protect 〜を保護する

One-up surround の使い方

surround は「〜を取り囲む」という他動詞ですが、surrounding は「取り囲んでいる、周囲の」という形容詞としてしばしば使われます。例えば surrounding area であれば「周辺地域」という意味になります。

よりぬき！テスト

解説

攻略法

トレーニング

確認テスト

解説

トレーニング

Questions 5-7 refer to the following coupon.

Arusa Café
Quality Coffee, Great Times

To celebrate the March reopening of our Fifth Street, Fakeham branch, ❶please use this beverage coupon ❷anytime until the end of May. ❸The coupon can be used on any standard menu item, excluding fresh juices and frozen yogurts.

❹This coupon can only be used with orders exceeding $10.00. There is a limit of one free beverage per coupon. ❺Further copies can be made by visiting our Web site. ❻This promotion applies only to the Fifth Street, Fakeham outlet of Arusa Café.

www.arusa-cafe.co.uk

問題 5-7 は次のクーポンに関するものです。

Arusa Café
上質なコーヒー、充実した時間

Fakeham 5 番通り店の 3 月の再オープンを祝し、5 月末までいつでも、このドリンククーポンをご利用ください。クーポンはフレッシュジュースとフローズンヨーグルトを除く、どの通常メニューの商品にもお使いいただけます。

このクーポンは 10 ドルを超えるご注文にのみお使いいただけます。クーポン 1 枚につき無料のお飲み物は 1 杯に限られます。当店のウェブサイトにアクセスし追加でコピーすることが可能です。このプロモーションは Arusa Café の Fakeham 5 番通りの店舗にのみ適用されます。

www.arusa-cafe.co.uk

┌─ 語句 ─────────────────────────────────────
│ □ quality 質の高い　□ celebrate 〜を祝う　□ reopening 再オープン
│ □ branch 支店　□ beverage 飲み物　□ anytime いつでも
│ □ until 〜までずっと　□ standard 標準　□ excluding 〜を除いて
│ □ exceed 〜を超える　□ limit 制限　□ free 無料の　□ per 〜につき
│ □ further さらなる　□ promotion 販売促進　□ apply to 〜に適用する
│ □ outlet 直販店、店舗
└──

5. For what can the coupon be used?

(A) An orange juice
(B) A dessert
(C) A soda
(D) A sandwich

このクーポンは何に対し利用できますか。

(A) オレンジジュース
(B) デザート
(C) ソーダ
(D) サンドイッチ

正解 C

解説

第1段落の❶に please use this beverage coupon「このドリンククーポンをご利用ください」とあるため、この時点で正解は (A) か (C) に絞られます。次に❸には The coupon can be used on any standard menu item, excluding fresh juices and frozen yogurts.「クーポンはフレッシュジュースとフローズンヨーグルトを除く、どの通常メニューの商品にもお使いいただけます」とあります。よって、正解は (C) になります。

❶本文→選択肢の言い換え

beverage ➡ orange juice, soda
fresh juices ➡ orange juice

One-up 前置詞の excluding

exclude は「〜を除く」という意味で使われる他動詞ですが、ing 形の excluding は動名詞、現在分詞以外にも前置詞として使われます。前置詞の excluding は「〜を除いて」という意味で、対義語は including「〜を含めて」（こちらも前置詞です）になります。

6. What is NOT true about the coupon offer?

    (A) It can be used in April.
    (B) Users must purchase other items.
    (C) More than one person can use it.
    (D) Additional coupons can be printed at home.

クーポン値引きに関し正しくないのはどれですか。

    (A) 4月に利用可能である。
    (B) 利用者は他の商品を購入しなければならない。
    (C) 複数人で利用できる。
    (D) 追加のクーポンを家で印刷できる。

正解 C

解説

(A) はクーポンの有効期間について第1段落の❷に anytime until the end of May「5月末までいつでも」とあり、(B) は第2段落の❹に This coupon can only be used with orders exceeding $10.00.「このクーポンは10ドルを超えるご注文にのみお使いいただけます」の部分が該当します。(D) は第2段落の❺に Further copies can be made by visiting our Web site.「当店のウェブサイトにアクセスし追加でコピーすることが可能です」とあることと一致しています。よって、正解は (C) です。

❶本文→選択肢の言い換え

(A) please use this beverage coupon anytime until the end of May ➡ It can be used in April.
(B) This coupon can only be used with orders exceeding $10.00. ➡ Users must purchase other items.
(D) Further copies can be made by visiting our Web site. ➡ Additional coupons can be printed at home.

□ offer 値引き　□ purchase ～を購入する　□ item 商品
□ more than ～より多い　□ person 人　□ additional 追加の
□ print ～を印刷する

7. What is implied about Arusa Café?

(A) It operates in multiple locations.
(B) It opened five years ago.
(C) It serves freshly-made food.
(D) It offers the coupon annually.

Arusa Café について何が示唆されていますか。

（A）複数の店舗で営業している。
（B）5年前に開店した。
（C）作りたての料理を提供する。
（D）1年に1度クーポンを提供する。

正解　A

解説

第2段落の ❻ に This promotion applies only to the Fifth Street, Fakeham outlet of Arusa Café. 「このプロモーションは Arusa Café の Fakeham 5番通りの店舗にのみ適用されます」とあります。このことから、Arusa Café は他にも店舗があることが推測されるため、正解は（A）です。

❗本文→選択肢の言い換え

applies only to the Fifth Street, Fakeham outlet of Arusa Café
➡ It operates in multiple locations.

語句

□ imply ～をほのめかす　□ operate 営業する　□ multiple 複数の
□ location 店舗　□ serve （食事や飲み物を）出す
□ freshly-made 作りたての　□ offer ～を提供する
□ annually 毎年、年に1回

Questions 8-11 refer to the following article.

What's Happening in Corkstone

CORKSTONE (July 10)— Residents going to Corkstone train station may want to rethink how they get there. ❶In line with the city's stated goal of reducing carbon emissions from local travel, ❷a new building for parking bicycles has opened beside the station. — [1] —.

City officials hope the free-to-use facility will encourage more citizens to cycle to the station. The building features secure parking, and the enclosed space protects bicycles from the weather. ❸The running costs will be partly funded by increased car parking charges around the station area. — [2] —. Although there is no charge, passes are needed to use the bicycle parking. This allows City Hall to monitor user numbers. ❹People can get one directly from the office at the facility's entrance. — [3] —.

Bicycle shop owner Liam Kane welcomed the policy. "It's a fantastic way to promote cycling. Bicycles are great for the earth and for your health." — [4] —. ❺Mayor Harrison commented, "We're seeing more and more families choosing to live in Corkstone, which is wonderful, but it must not lead to increased traffic on our roads. Journeys made by bicycle have a part to play in keeping cars off the road."

問題 8-11 は次の記事に関するものです。

Corkstone で何が起きているか

CORKSTONE（7月10日） ― Corkstone 駅へ行く住人は、そこへの行き方をもう一度考えてみてもよいかもしれない。市が発表した地域交通からの炭素排出削減の目標に従い、自転車を停めるための新しい建物が駅の隣にオープンした。― [1] ―

市の職員は、無料の施設があることでより多くの市民に駅までの自転車利用を促すことを望んでいる。この建物は安全な駐輪が特徴となっており、閉鎖的空間が天候から自転車を守る。運営費用は駅周辺の地域で増加した駐車料金によって一部賄われる。― [2] ― この駐輪場の利用は無料だが、許可証は必要である。これにより市役所は利用者番号を管理できるようになる。許可証は施設の入り口にある事務所から直接入手できる。― [3] ―

自転車販売店の店主 Liam Kane はこの方針を歓迎した。「自転車の利用を促進する素晴らしい方法です。地球のためにも健康のためにも、自転車は優れています。」― [4] ― Harrison 市長は次のようにコメントした。「ますます多くの家族が Corkstone での暮らしを選ぶようになっており、これは素晴らしいことですが、道路交通量の増加につなげてはいけません。自転車での移動は車の交通量を抑える上で重要な役割があります。」

よりぬき！テスト

解説

攻略法

トレーニング

確認テスト

解説

トレーニング

□ resident 住民　□ rethink 〜を再考する　□ in line with 〜に従って

□ reduce 〜を減らす　□ carbon emission 炭素排出　□ local 地元の

□ beside 〜のそばに、〜の横に　□ city official 市の職員

□ free-to-use 無料で使える　□ facility 施設

□ encourage somebody to do 人が〜するのを促す　□ citizen 市民

□ cycle to 〜に自転車で行く　□ feature 〜を呼び物にする、〜を特徴とする

□ secure 安全な　□ enclose 〜を囲む　□ protect 〜を保護する

□ running cost 運営費　□ partly 部分的には　□ fund 〜に資金を与える

□ increase 増える　□ charge 料金、使用料　□ although 〜だけれども

□ allow something to do 物が〜できるようにする　□ City Hall 市役所

□ monitor 〜を監視する、〜を管理する　□ directly 直接

□ entrance 入り口　□ welcome 〜を歓迎する　□ policy 方針

□ fantastic 素晴らしい　□ promote 〜を促進する　□ mayor 市長

□ lead to 〜につながる

□ have a part to play in 〜で重要な役割を担っている

□ keep something off 物を〜から遠ざける

8. What does the article discuss?

(A) A city's environmental policy
(B) The launch of a public transport network
(C) New ways to attract families to a city
(D) Improvements to a train station building

この記事では何が述べられていますか。

(A) 市の環境方針
(B) 公共交通網の発足
(C) ファミリー層を市へ誘致する新たな方法
(D) 駅舎の改良

正解 **A**

解説

第1段落の ❶ に In line with the city's stated goal of reducing carbon emissions from local travel「市が発表した地域交通からの炭素排出削減の目標に従い」とあるため、これを抽象的に言い換えている（A）が正解です。

❶本文→選択肢の言い換え

city's stated goal of reducing carbon emissions from local travel
➡ city's environmental policy

語句
□ discuss ～について述べる　□ environmental 環境の
□ launch 開始、立ち上げ　□ public transport network 公共交通網
□ attract A to B　AをBに引きつける　□ improvement to ～の改良
□ station building 駅舎

9. Where can passes be obtained?

(A) At City Hall
(B) In local bicycle shops
(C) In the station ticket office
(D) Next to the station

許可証はどこで入手できますか。

(A) 市役所
(B) 地元の自転車販売店
(C) 駅の切符売り場
(D) 駅の隣

正解 D

解説

第1段落の**❷**に a new building for parking bicycles has opened beside the station「自転車を停めるための新しい建物が駅の隣にオープンした」とあります。また、第2段落の**❹**に People can get one directly from the office at the facility's entrance.「人々は施設の入り口にある事務所から直接それ（許可証）を入手できる」とあります。駅の隣にオープンした施設の入り口にある事務所で許可証は手に入るので、正解は（D）です。

❗本文→選択肢の言い換え

beside the station ➡ Next to the station
People can get one (=pass) ➡ passes can be obtained

語句
□ obtain ～を手に入れる　□ next to ～の隣に

よりぬき！テスト

解説

攻略法

トレーニング

確認テスト

解説

トレーニング

10. What did Mayor Harrison imply about Corkstone?

(A) It needs to attract investments.

(B) Citizens are not happy with travel charges.

(C) Its population is rising.

(D) Car drivers should be more careful.

Harrison 市長は Corkstone について何を示唆しましたか。

(A) 投資を誘致する必要がある。

(B) 市民は交通料金に満足していない。

(C) 人口が増加している。

(D) 車の運転手はもっと注意すべきである。

正解 C

解説

第3段落の❺に Mayor Harrison commented, "We're seeing more and more families choosing to live in Corkstone 「Harrison 市長は次のようにコメントした。『ますます多くの家族が Corkstone での暮らしを選ぶようになっている』」とあります。よって、正解は (C) です。

❶ 本文→選択肢の言い換え

We're seeing more and more families choosing to live in Corkstone ➡ Its population is rising.

語句

□ imply 〜をほのめかす　□ attract 〜を引きつける　□ investment 投資

□ population 人口　□ rise 上がる　□ careful 注意深い

11. In which of the positions marked [1], [2], [3], and [4] does the following sentence best belong?

"It is hoped that the fees will further push people to change their habits."

(A) [1]
(B) [2]
(C) [3]
(D) [4]

[1]、[2]、[3] および [4] と記載された箇所のうち、次の文が入るのに最もふさわしいのはどれですか。

「この料金が人々の習慣を変える後押しになることが期待される。」

(A) [1]
(B) [2]
(C) [3]
(D) [4]

正解 **B**

解説

挿入する文にある「この料金が人々の習慣を変える後押しになることが期待される」という内容から、正解の位置の前後には「料金」に関する話題があると推測することができます。第2段落の❸に The running costs will be partly funded by increased car parking charges around the station area.「運営費用は駅周辺の地域で増加した駐車料金によって一部賄われる」とあります。❸より前も、無料の駐輪場があることで人々が利用する交通手段が車から自転車に変わることを見通す内容が書かれています。よって、正解は (B) です。(A) や (C)、(D) の前後には、上記のような「料金」に関する話題はありません。

❶本文→挿入文の言い換え

increased car parking charges around the station area
➡ the fees

（**語句**）
☐ fee　料金　　☐ further　さらに
☐ push somebody to do　人が〜するよう駆り立てる　　☐ habit　習慣

Questions 12-15 refer to the following online chat discussion.

Michelle Groves [10:20 A.M.]: Good morning Anna and Pascal. Most of the details of your catering order have been finalized. I'll be making the necessary purchases today and tomorrow. ❶I just need to confirm whether there are any dietary needs or not.

Anna Nakamura [10:22 A.M.]: Hi Michelle. What do you mean exactly?

Michelle Groves [10:23 A.M.]: ❷For example, some people may be allergic to nuts or perhaps some do not eat meat.

Anna Nakamura [10:25 A.M.]: ❸I get you. Pascal will know that better than me. Pascal?

Pascal Levant [10:28 A.M.]: No one has mentioned anything to me.

Michelle Groves [10:30 A.M.]: OK. I'm planning to top the cake with nuts, so I'll go ahead with that. And there will some basic vegetarian dishes anyway.

Anna Nakamura [10:31 A.M.]: Good to know. What time can we expect you to arrive on the 23rd?

Michelle Groves [10:33 A.M.]: Around 11. That reminds me – will it be possible to leave my van near the main entrance? ❹I have a lot of things to unload, and I'd rather not carry them too far.

Anna Nakamura [10:36 A.M.]: Leave it to me. I'll make sure there's a space for you.

Pascal Levant [10:38 A.M.]: And I'll be there to greet you when you arrive. ❺Everything needs to be perfect for our German colleagues. We want them to experience some genuine American hospitality!

問題 12-15 は次のオンラインチャットの話し合いに関するものです。

よりぬき！テスト

Michelle Groves［午前 10 時 20 分］：Anna、Pascal、おはようございます。あなた方のケータリング注文について細かな点の大部分が最終決定に入っています。今日と明日で必要な買い物をします。ただ食事に関する要望があるかどうか確認したいのですが。

Anna Nakamura［午前 10 時 22 分］：こんにちは、Michelle。厳密にはどういうことですか。

Michelle Groves［午前 10 時 23 分］：例えば、ナッツにアレルギーがある人がいるかもしれないとか、あるいは、おそらく肉を食さない人がいるとか。

Anna Nakamura［午前 10 時 25 分］：なるほど。それについては私より Pascal の方が知っていると思います。Pascal ？

Pascal Levant［午前 10 時 28 分］：私には誰も何も言ってきていません。

Michelle Groves［午前 10 時 30 分］：分かりました。ケーキの上にナッツをのせる予定でいますが、それで進めます。それからどのみちベジタリアン用の基本的な料理はあります。

Anna Nakamura［午前 10 時 31 分］：いいですね。23 日は何時に到着できそうですか。

Michelle Groves［午前 10 時 33 分］：11 時頃です。そういえば、正面玄関の近くに私の小型トラックを停めても大丈夫ですか。降ろす荷物が多くて、できればあまり遠い距離を運びたくないのです。

Anna Nakamura［午前 10 時 36 分］：私に任せてください。駐車スペースを確保しておきます。

Pascal Levant［午前 10 時 38 分］：それにあなたが到着するときにそこで出迎えます。ドイツからやってくる同僚たちに対して全て完璧でなくてはなりません。アメリカの本当のおもてなしを彼らに体験してもらいたいですから！

190

12. What does Ms. Groves want to confirm?

(A) The size of the order
(B) The final cost of the event
(C) The type of ingredients
(D) The number of attendees

Groves さんが確認したいことは何ですか。

(A) 注文の量
(B) イベントの最終的な費用
(C) 材料の種類
(D) 参加者数

正解 C

解説

午前 10 時 20 分の Groves さんの発言に、❶ I just need to confirm whether there are any dietary needs or not.「ただ食事に関する要望があるかどうか確認したいのですが」とあります。また、午前 10 時 23 分の発言では ❷ For example, some people may be allergic to nuts or perhaps some do not eat meat.「例えば、ナッツにアレルギーがある人がいるかもしれないとか、あるいは、おそらく肉を食さない人がいるとか」とあります。これらから、Groves さんはケータリング注文の食事内容を確認したいと考えていることが分かります。よって、正解は（C）です。

❶ 本文→選択肢の言い換え

whether there are any dietary needs or not
➡ The type of ingredients

語句
□ confirm ～を確認する　□ ingredient 材料　□ attendee 参加者

他動詞の attend は「～に出席する」という意味ですが、派生語も含めて TOEIC L&R テストでは頻出なので、ここでまとめて大切なことを押さえておいてください。

① attend「～に出席する」：他動詞
　　attend ≒ take part in、participate in、join
② attendee「出席者」：可算名詞
③ attendance「出席」：不可算名詞、「出席者数」：可算名詞
　　Attendance at the seminar is by invitation only.
　　「セミナーへの出席はご招待された方に限ります」
　　There was a large attendance at the conference.
　　「会議は出席者多数でした」

13. At 10:28 A.M., what does Mr. Levant most likely mean when he writes, "No one has mentioned anything to me"?

(A) Special options are not required.

(B) Ms. Groves should wait for a response.

(C) He is surprised at a menu item.

(D) His previous cost estimate was correct.

午前 10 時 28 分に、Levant さんが "No one has mentioned anything to me" と書く際、何を意図していると考えられますか。

（A）特別なオプションは必要とされていない。

（B）Groves さんは返答を待つべきである。

（C）彼はメニューの品に驚いている。

（D）彼の以前の費用見積額は正しかった。

正解　**A**

解説

Groves さんがケータリング注文の食事内容についてアレルギーや好みの要望がきているかを Anna と Pascal に尋ねると、午前 10 時 25 分に Anna Nakamura さんは❸ I get you. Pascal will know that better than me. Pascal?「なるほど。それについては私より Pascal の方が知っていると思います。Pascal ？」と発言しています。これに対する応答なので、Pascal Levant さんは <u>No one has mentioned anything to me</u>「（ケータリングを届ける先の）誰も（特に食事内容に関する要望は）何も言ってきていない」と伝えている訳です。食材について特別な配慮は不要なので、正解は（A）です。

❶ 本文→選択肢の言い換え

No one has mentioned anything

➡ Special options are not required.

語句
- □ option 選択肢、オプション　□ require ～を必要とする
- □ wait for ～を待つ　□ response 応答　□ be surprised at ～に驚く
- □ previous 以前の　□ estimate 見積もり　□ correct 正しい

14. What is Ms. Groves concerned about?

(A) She may not have enough food containers.
(B) She may require help to unload her vehicle.
(C) She may not have enough time to set up.
(D) She may need to park some distance from the venue.

Groves さんは何を心配していますか。

(A) 十分な食品容器がないかもしれない。
(B) 車から荷物を降ろすのに手伝いを要するかもしれない。
(C) 準備のための十分な時間がないかもしれない。
(D) 会場から少し離れたところに駐車する必要があるかもしれない。

正解 D

解説

午前 10 時 33 分の発言で、Groves さんは❹ I have a lot of things to unload, and I'd rather not carry them too far.「降ろす荷物が多くて、できればあまり遠い距離を運びたくないのです」と述べています。ケータリングを行う場所から遠いところに車を停めるのは避けたいと考えていることが分かるため、正解は (D) です。

❶本文→選択肢の言い換え

carry them（= a lot of things to unload）too far
　➡ park some distance from the venue

┌ **語句** ┄┄┄┄┄┄┄┄┄┄┄┄┄┄┄┄┄┄┄┄┄┄┄┄┄┄┄┄┄┄┄┄┄┄
│ ☐ be concerned about ～について心配する　☐ container 容器
│ ☐ vehicle 乗り物　☐ set up （食事などを）用意する
│ ☐ park some distance from ～から少し距離のあるところに駐車する
│ ☐ venue 会場
└┄┄

15. Why most likely is the event being held?

(A) A manager is going to retire.
(B) Overseas staff will visit the company.
(C) A new product will be launched.
(D) A European branch office will open.

イベントはなぜ開催されると考えられますか。

(A) マネージャーが退職する。
(B) 海外のスタッフが会社を訪れる。
(C) 新しい製品が発売される。
(D) ヨーロッパ支社がオープンする。

正解 **B**

解説

午前10時38分のLevantさんの発言に、❺ Everything needs to be perfect for our German colleagues. 「ドイツからやってくる同僚たちに対して全て完璧でなくてはなりません」とあります。よって、正解は（B）です。

❶ 本文→選択肢の言い換え

German colleagues ➡ overseas staff

語句
☐ be held 開催される　☐ retire 退職する　☐ overseas 海外の
☐ product 製品　☐ launch ～を発売する　☐ branch office 支店

One-up 「行われる」を表す表現

「行われる、開催される」は、be held や take place を使って表しますが、これらは登場頻度が非常に高い表現です。いずれも「主語」が開催されることを表すときに使います。
The competition will be held next month.
「大会は来月開催予定です」

Questions 16-20 refer to the following article and e-mail.

19 April — ❶Vue Garden Hotel Group will open another hotel in Pattaya later this year, which will bring much-needed jobs to the area. ❷The hotel will have 150 rooms along with formal meeting facilities, as Vue Garden hopes to attract business travelers as well as traditional vacationers. ❸Unlike the group's existing hotel in the town, ❹this one will feature exclusive access to a 100-meter stretch of beach to enjoy swimming in the bay's crystal clear waters. ❺Plans also show an upscale dining option, a gym and sauna, and an event hall.

People wishing to apply for a position at the hotel, which will open in October, should visit the group's Web site and complete the job application form. According to a Vue Garden statement, people with experience in customer service or room cleaning are especially needed. However, ❻the group is looking to hire young people with no previous work experience as part of their kitchen crew in order to train them in Vue Garden's unique cooking methods. ❼The application deadline is July 1, with training for new employees beginning one month later.

問題 16-20 は次の記事と E メールに関するものです。

4月19日 － Vue Garden Hotel Group は、今年中に Pattaya にホテルをもう一軒オープンする予定で、切望されている雇用がその地域にもたらされるでしょう。ホテルには 150 の客室、それに正式な会議を行える施設を備える予定で、Vue Garden は従来の行楽客だけでなくビジネス旅行者の取り込みも望んでいます。町にあるこのグループの既存のホテルとは異なり、このホテルは、100 メートルにわたる専用ビーチを利用できるのが売りで、入り江の澄み渡る水での海水浴を楽しむことができます。計画はまた、高級なレストラン、ジムとサウナ、そしてイベ

ントホールを含むとしています。

10月に開業予定の、このホテルの求人に応募を望む方は、グループのウェブサイトにアクセスし仕事の応募フォームに記入する必要があります。Vue Garden の発表によると、顧客サービスまたは客室清掃の経験者が特に必要とされています。しかしグループは、過去に仕事の経験がない若者をキッチンクルーの一員として雇用し Vue Garden 独特の料理法をトレーニングしようと考えています。応募締め切りは 7 月 1 日で、新しい従業員のための研修は 1 カ月後に始まります。

【語句】

□ another もう一つの　□ later this year 今年中に　□ bring 〜をもたらす
□ much-needed 待ち望まれている　□ along with 〜と一緒に
□ formal 正式な　□ facility 施設　□ attract 〜を引きつける
□ A as well as B　B だけでなく A も　□ traditional 昔ながらの、従来の
□ vacationer 行楽客　□ unlike 〜とは違って　□ existing 既存の
□ feature 〜を目玉にする　□ exclusive 独占的な
□ access to 〜へのアクセス　□ stretch 長さ　□ bay 湾、入り江
□ crystal clear 澄み渡った　□ upscale 高級な　□ apply for 〜に応募する
□ position 職、仕事の口　□ complete 〜を完成させる、〜に記入する
□ application 申し込み、応募　□ according to 〜によると
□ statement 声明　□ experience 経験　□ especially 特に
□ look to do 〜しようとする　□ hire 〜を雇う　□ previous 以前の
□ as 〜として　□ crew クルー、（一緒に仕事をする）チーム
□ in order to do 〜するために　□ train 〜を訓練する　□ unique 独特な
□ method 方法　□ employee 従業員　□ later 後で

To:	Ally Thongsuk <happyally@usendmail.com>
From:	Henri Poll <poll.h@vuegardenhotel.com>
Date:	5 July
Subject:	Job application
Attachment:	Information

Dear Ms. Thongsuk,

Thank you for completing an online application for our new hotel in Pattaya. After careful consideration, ❽we would like you to attend an interview to discuss your desire to join us as a junior kitchen assistant. ❾Interviews will be held at Quantum Business Park on 14 July. Please see the attached information for directions and times. There is a frequent public bus service to the park.

We expect all applicants to arrive on time and to be formally dressed. As the interview will take place over two sessions, ❿a complimentary lunch will be provided. As preparation for the interview, we hope you can research Vue Garden's mission statement and history. These can be found on our Web site.

Warmest regards,

Henri Poll
Assistant Manager

宛先：Ally Thongsuk <happyally@usendmail.com>
送信者：Henri Poll <poll.h@vuegardenhotel.com>
日付：7月5日
件名：仕事への応募
添付：資料

Thongsuk 様

Pattaya の新ホテルへのオンライン応募にご記入いただきありがとうございます。検討の結果、ジュニア・キッチン・アシスタントとして私たちの仲間に加わりたいと希望されていることについて話し合うために、あなたに面接に参加していただきたいと考えています。面接は7月14日に Quantum Business Park にて行われます。道順や日程に関し添付の資料をご確認ください。公園へ向かう公共バスは頻繁に走っています。

応募者の皆さんは時間厳守かつ正装でお越しください。面接は2回にわたって行われますので、無料の昼食が提供されます。面接の準備として、Vue Garden の企業理念と歴史を調べていただくとよいでしょう。当社のウェブサイトでご覧いただけます。

よろしくお願いいたします。

アシスタントマネージャー
Henri Poll

語句

□ attachment 添付ファイル　□ information 情報、資料
□ thank you for doing 〜してくれてありがとう　□ careful 注意深い
□ consideration 考慮　□ would like somebody to do 人に〜してほしい
□ attend 〜に参加する　□ interview 面接　□ discuss 〜について話す
□ desire 望み　□ be held 行われる　□ attached 添付されている
□ direction 道順　□ frequent 頻繁な
□ expect somebody to do 人が〜するのを期待する　□ applicant 応募者
□ on time 時間どおりに　□ formally dressed 正装をしている
□ as 〜なので　□ take place 行われる　□ complimentary 無料の
□ provide 〜を提供する　□ preparation for 〜の準備
□ research 〜を調査する　□ mission statement （企業）理念
□ Warmest regards, よろしくお願いいたします。

16. What is true of Vue Garden's new hotel?

(A) It will be built on the site of an existing hotel.
(B) It will be the group's second branch in Pattaya.
(C) It will focus on luxury guest rooms.
(D) It will likely open ahead of schedule.

Vue Garden の新しいホテルについて正しいのはどれですか。

(A) 既存のホテルの土地に建てられる。
(B) Pattaya ではグループの 2 番目の支店である。
(C) 豪華な客室に注力する。
(D) 予定より早くオープンする可能性が高い。

正解 B

解説

1 つ目の文書の第 1 段落の❶に、Vue Garden Hotel Group will open another hotel in Pattaya later this year「Vue Garden Hotel Group は、今年中に Pattaya にホテルをもう一軒オープンする予定です」とあります。また、❸では Unlike the group's existing hotel in the town「町にあるこのグループの既存のホテルとは異なり」と述べられ、hotel が単数形であるため、これらから Pattaya にオープンするホテルは 2 つ目のホテルになることが分かります。よって、正解は（B）です。

❗本文→選択肢の言い換え

will open another hotel in Pattaya

➡ will be the group's second branch in Pattaya

語句

□ site 場所 □ branch 支店 □ focus on ～に焦点を当てる
□ luxury 贅沢な □ ahead of schedule 予定より早く

17. What will NOT be a facility of the hotel?

(A) A private beach
(B) A fitness center
(C) A swimming pool
(D) Conference rooms

ホテルの施設でないのはどれですか。

(A) プライベートビーチ
(B) フィットネスセンター
(C) スイミングプール
(D) 会議室

正解 C

解説

(A) は 1 つ目の文書の第 1 段落の❹ this one will feature exclusive access to a 100-meter stretch of beach 「このホテルは、100 メートルにわたる専用ビーチを利用できるのが売りです」に、(B) は❺の Plans also show an upscale dining option, a gym and sauna, and an event hall. 「計画はまた、高級なレストラン、ジムとサウナ、そしてイベントホールを含むとしています」に、そして (D) は❷の The hotel will have 150 rooms along with formal meeting facilities 「ホテルには 150 の客室、それに正式な会議を行える施設を備える予定です」とあります。スイミングプールに関してはどこにも述べられていないため、正解は (C) です。

●本文→選択肢の言い換え

(A) exclusive access to a 100-meter stretch of beach
　➡ A private beach
(B) a gym ➡ A fitness center
(D) formal meeting facilities ➡ Conference rooms

語句
□ private 個人用の　□ conference 会議

18. What will happen in August?

(A) Staff will receive training.
(B) Interviews will be held.
(C) The hotel will accept bookings.
(D) A promotional event will take place.

8月に何がありますか。

(A) スタッフが研修を受ける。
(B) 面接が行われる。
(C) ホテルが予約を受け付ける。
(D) 販売促進イベントが行われる。

正解 A

解説

1つ目の文書の第2段落の❼に、The application deadline is July 1, with training for new employees beginning one month later.「応募締め切りは7月1日で、新しい従業員のための研修は1カ月後に始まります」とあります。7月1日の1カ月後、つまり8月に従業員の研修が始まることが分かるので、正解は（A）です。

❶本文→選択肢の言い換え

July 1, one month later ➡ August
employees ➡ staff

語句

□ happen 起こる　□ receive ～を受ける　□ accept ～を受け入れる
□ booking 予約　□ promotional 販売を促進する

One-up 説明は「後ろから」

どんなに長い文であったとしても、英語は常に「左から右に」流れていきます。後ろに続くものが前にあるものを説明するのです。⑦の長めの文も、前から順を追って意味を取っていけば容易に理解できるはずです。

The application deadline is July 1,「応募締め切りは 7 月 1 日です」
（どういうものが続くのかというと）
→ with training「研修があります」
（誰のための研修かというと）
→ for new employees「新しい従業員のための研修です」
（いつから始まるのかというと）
→ beginning one month later.「1 カ月後に始まります」

19. What is implied about Ms. Thongsuk?

(A) She already met Mr. Poll.
(B) She will deal with hotel guests.
(C) She was late in sending her application.
(D) She has never worked in a hotel.

Thongsuk さんについて何が示唆されていますか。

(A) 彼女は Poll 氏にすでに会っている。
(B) 彼女はホテルの宿泊客に対応する。
(C) 彼女は応募書類の送付が遅かった。
(D) 彼女はホテルで働いたことがない。

正解 **D**

1つ目の文書の第2段落の❻に the group is looking to hire young people with no previous work experience as part of their kitchen crew「グループは、過去に仕事の経験がない若者をキッチンクルーの一員として雇用しようと考えています」とあります。また、2つ目の文書（Thongsuk さん宛のEメール）の第1段落の❽に、we would like you to attend an interview to discuss your desire to join us as a junior kitchen assistant「ジュニア・キッチン・アシスタントとして私たちの仲間に加わりたいと希望されていることについて話し合うために、あなたに面接に参加していただきたいと考えています」とあります。これらのことから、Thongsuk さんはホテルのキッチンで働きたいと考えていて、この職は未経験者の採用も行われるということが分かります。よって、正解は（D）です。

❗本文→選択肢の言い換え

no previous work experience ➡ never worked

□ imply 〜をほのめかす　□ already すでに　□ deal with 〜に対応する
□ application 応募書類

One-up look to do と look to ＋名詞

look を使った表現は、look at「〜を見る」や look forward to doing / 名詞「〜（するの）を楽しみに待つ」などがありますが、look to do と look to ＋名詞も使いこなせるよう、ここでまとめて覚えておきましょう。

① look to do 「〜しようとする」、「〜することを目指す」
　Our company is looking to cut costs.
　「私たちの会社はコスト削減を目指しています」
② look to ＋名詞 「〜を頼る」、「〜に期待している」
　The employees in this company look to the new CEO.
　「この会社の従業員は、新しい CEO に期待している」

20. What will be provided at Quantum Business Park?

(A) Complimentary transportation
(B) An information packet
(C) A free meal
(D) Staff uniforms

Quantum Business Park で何が提供されますか。

(A) 無料の交通
(B) 資料一式
(C) 無料の食事
(D) スタッフ用の制服

正解 C

解説

2つ目の文書の第1段落の❾に、Interviews will be held at Quantum Business Park on 14 July.「面接は7月14日に Quantum Business Park にて行われます」とあり、第2段落の❿には a complimentary lunch will be provided「無料の昼食が提供されます」とあります。面接会場である Quantum Business Park では無料の昼食が出るということが分かるため、正解は（C）です。

❶本文→選択肢の言い換え

a complimentary lunch ➡ A free meal

語句
□ transportation 輸送（機関）　□ packet 包み　□ free 無料の
□ meal 食事

Questions 21-25 refer to the following e-mail, brochure, and notice.

From:	human.resources@tvb-insurance.com
To:	dewan.v@tvb-insurance.com
Date:	9 September
Subject:	Reach Out courses

Dear Vikram Dewan,

We at Human Resources received notification through your section head, Paula Ingram, of ❶your interest in completing a course at our training partner, Reach Out Education. ❷We will be delighted to support you in your wish to improve and update your first aid skills. This will benefit not only you, but those around you if there is ever an accident or injury in the office. After finishing the course, we may ask you to run an informal workshop for your colleagues to pass on your skills.

The course will be held at Reach Out's office in central Leeds on every Tuesday in October and November. Needless to say, you will be given paid time off to attend the course, and ❸all fees will be covered by TVB Insurance.

I will forward you further information as I receive it from Reach Out.

Sally Milligan
Head of Human Resources

問題 21-25 は次の E メール、パンフレット、お知らせに関するものです。

送信者：human.resources@tvb-insurance.com
宛先：dewan.v@tvb-insurance.com
日付：9 月 9 日
件名：Reach Out コース

Vikram Dewan 様

人事部は、あなたが当社の研修パートナーである Reach Out Education で講座を履修することに興味があるとの通知を、あなたの課の Paula Ingram 課長を通して受け取りました。私たちは、応急処置技能を向上させ最新のものにしたいというあなたを喜んでサポートします。これはあなたのためだけでなく、万が一事務所で事故や怪我が生じた場合にあなたの周りの人のためにもなります。このコースの修了後、同僚に向けてそのスキルを伝授する非公式のワークショップの実施をお願いするかもしれません。

このコースは 10 月と 11 月の毎週火曜日に Leeds の中心部にある Reach Out の事務所で行われます。言うまでもありませんが、コースの出席に関し有給休暇が与えられ、授業料は全て TVB Insurance が負担します。

詳しい情報は Reach Out から受け取り次第転送します。

人事部長
Sally Milligan

語句

□ notification 通知　□ through ～を通して　□ section 課、部門
□ interest in ～への関心　□ complete ～を完成させる
□ be delighted to do 喜んで～する　□ support ～を支える　□ wish 願い
□ improve ～を改良する　□ update ～を最新のものにする
□ first aid 応急処置　□ benefit ～に恩恵を与える、～のためになる
□ not only A but B A だけでなく B に　□ those 人々　□ injury 怪我
□ run ～を運営する　□ informal 非公式の　□ colleague 同僚
□ pass on ～を伝える　□ needless to say 言うまでもなく
□ paid time off 有給休暇　□ attend ～に参加する　□ fee 料金、授業料
□ cover （費用を）負担する　□ forward ～に送る　□ as ～する際に
□ Human Resources 人事部

Reach Out Education
32-35 Hanover St.
Leeds LS2 9OL
Tel: (0133) 555-4040

Reach Out Education's classroom-based courses cover a wide variety of topics aimed at those in work, in education, or searching for employment. Passing one of our programs means you'll leave with a nationally-recognized qualification to boost your career prospects. With maximum class sizes of fifteen people, ❹each student has plenty of time with both their lead course instructor and assistant teacher.

October-November Class Offerings on Workplace Safety

Hygiene
For food preparation staff. Learn the essentials of safe food handling techniques and cleanliness in order to prevent sickness and to comply with national laws.

Fire Safety
This class covers what to do in a fire emergency. Learn how to act, how to direct colleagues to safety, and basic survival skills. You'll also learn fire prevention strategies.

Working Smart
Study techniques on avoiding common workplace injuries that often happen when lifting heavy items or not using the correct equipment. This can lead to a CityTec qualification in workplace safety.

❺Quick Response
❻Learn how to deal with a variety of medical emergencies before the professionals arrive. Your quick actions could save the life of a colleague. The course covers basic biology, covering wounds, and treating shock.

Reach Out Education

32-35 Hanover St.
Leeds LS2 9OL
電話：(0133) 555-4040

Reach Out Education の教室中心のコースは、就業者、教育従事者、また求職中の方々を対象に、様々なテーマを網羅しています。プログラムを一つ修了すれば、キャリアアップの強みとなる全国的に認められた資格を持って卒業することになります。クラスの定員数は 15 名で、各生徒はコースの主任講師とアシスタント講師の両方と十分な時間を過ごします。

10 月 -11 月の労働安全に関する授業の内容

衛生学
食品調理スタッフ向け。食中毒を予防し国内法令を遵守するための食品の安全な取り扱い方法および清浄について要点を学びます。

火災安全
この授業は火災緊急時にすべきことを網羅します。どのように行動し、どのように同僚を安全な場所へ誘導するか、そして生き残るための基本的技術を学びます。また、火災予防戦略も学びます。

賢い働き方
重いものを持ち上げるときや正しい器具を使わないときに起こりがちな、職場でよく見受けられる怪我を避けるための技術を学びます。これは労働安全の CityTec 資格に通じるものです。

迅速な対応
専門家が到着する前にどのように様々な医療的緊急事態に対処すべきかを学びます。あなたが迅速な対応をすることで同僚の命を救えるかもしれません。このコースは基礎生物学、傷の保護、ショック状態の手当てなどを扱います。

210

よりぬき！テスト

解説

攻略法

トレーニング

確認テスト

解説

トレーニング

NOTICE

The policy on payments for textbooks has changed. Course fees will no longer include the cost of course materials. Please pay for your textbooks on the day of your first class by going to the student affairs office on the first floor. Remember to bring your student identification number. ❼This does not <u>apply to</u> those whose fees are being paid by their employer. ❽In such cases, kindly collect an invoice from student affairs and give it to the relevant person in your workplace. Students repeating courses should check with their lead instructor to confirm that the course materials are unchanged.

お知らせ

教科書の支払いに関する方針が変わりました。コースの授業料は教材費を含まなくなります。授業の初日に１階の学生課へ行き教科書代をお支払いください。学生証番号を忘れずに提示してください。これは雇用主によって授業料を支払われている方々には適用されません。この場合、お手数ですが学生課から請求書を受け取り、職場の担当者にお渡しください。コースを再履修する学生は、コースの教材に変更がないか主任講師に確認してください。

語句

- □ notice お知らせ □ policy 方針 □ payment 支払い
- □ textbook 教科書 □ no longer もはや〜ではない □ include 〜を含む
- □ course material 教材 □ pay for 〜の支払いをする
- □ by doing 〜をすることによって □ student affairs office 学生課
- □ remember to do 忘れずに〜する □ identification 識別、本人確認
- □ apply to 〜に適用される □ employer 雇用主 □ kindly どうか〜
- □ collect 〜を受け取る □ invoice 請求書 □ relevant person 担当者
- □ check with 〜に確認をする □ confirm 〜を確認する
- □ unchanged 変更がない

21. Why was the e-mail sent?

(A) To ask for proof of qualifications
(B) To give advice on scheduling a course
(C) To request help running a workshop
(D) To approve a request for training

このEメールが送られたのはなぜですか。

(A) 資格証明書を求めるため
(B) コースの予定計画について助言するため
(C) ワークショップを実施する支援を求めるため
(D) 研修の要望を承認するため

正解 D

解説

1つ目の文書 (Dewan さん宛のEメール) の❶に your interest in completing a course「講座を履修することへのあなたの興味」とあり、❷には We will be delighted to support you in your wish to improve and update your first aid skills.「私たちは、応急処置技能を向上させ最新のものにしたいというあなたを喜んでサポートします」とあります。講座に参加したいと考えている Dewan さんを、会社は前向きに支持することを述べているため、正解は (D) です。

❗本文→選択肢の言い換え

interest in completing a course ➡ request for training
be delighted to support ➡ approve

語句
□ ask for ～を求める □ proof 証拠 □ schedule ～の予定を決める
□ request ～を求める □ approve ～を承認する □ request 要求
□ training 研修

22. What is indicated about courses at Reach Out Education?

(A) Each is conducted by two teaching staff members.

(B) Some are free of charge for unemployed people.

(C) They feature some online lessons.

(D) They take place in multiple locations.

Reach Out Education でのコースについて何が示されていますか。

(A) それぞれが 2 名の講師によって実施される。

(B) いくつかは失業者に対し無料である。

(C) いくつかのオンライン授業を特徴としている。

(D) 複数の場所で行われる。

正解 A

解説

2 つ目の文書（Reach Out Education のパンフレット）の❹に each student has plenty of time with both their lead course instructor and assistant teacher「各生徒はコースの主任講師とアシスタント講師の両方と十分な時間を過ごします」とあるため、各コースには 2 人の講師がいることが分かります。よって、正解は (A) です。

❶本文→選択肢の言い換え

with both their lead course instructor and assistant teacher

➡ conducted by two teaching staff members

語句

☐ indicate ～を示す　☐ each それぞれ　☐ conduct ～を行う

☐ free of charge 無料で　☐ unemployed 失業中の

☐ feature ～を目玉とする、～を特徴とする　☐ online オンラインの

☐ take place 行われる　☐ multiple 複数の　☐ location 場所

よりぬき！テスト

解説

攻略法

トレーニング

確認テスト

解説

トレーニング

each の使い方

> each は「それぞれの」という意味の形容詞、「それぞれ」という意味の名詞として使われる単語です。形容詞として後ろに続く名詞を修飾する場合、名詞は可算名詞の単数形になります。each、every、another という3つの形容詞は、後ろに名詞が続く場合、いずれもその名詞は単数形になると覚えておいてください。

---

23. What course will Mr. Dewan take?

(A) Hygiene
(B) Fire Safety
(C) Working Smart
(D) Quick Response

Dewan 氏はどのコースを取りますか。

(A) 衛生学
(B) 火災安全
(C) 賢い働き方
(D) 迅速な対応

正解　D

解説

1つ目の文書（Dewan さん宛のEメール）の❷に、We will be delighted to support you in your wish to improve and update your first aid skills. 「私たちは、応急処置技能を向上させ最新のものにしたいというあなたを喜んでサポートします」とあります。また、2つ目の文書（講座の内容を示すパンフレット）の❺には Quick Response「迅速な対応」、❻には Learn how to deal with a variety of medical emergencies before the professionals arrive.「専門家が到着する前にどのように様々な医療的緊急事態に対処すべきかを学びます」とあります。これらのことから、Dewan さんが参加すると考えられる講座は (D) です。

❶文書間の言い換え

improve and update your first aid skills

　➡ Learn how to deal with a variety of medical emergencies

語句
□ take　〜を取る

---

24. What does Mr. Dewan need to do regarding his course books?

(A) Pass a bill to his employer
(B) Buy course materials from a bookstore
(C) Pay at the student affairs office
(D) Talk to his course instructor

Dewan 氏は教科書について何をする必要がありますか。

(A) 請求書を雇用主に渡す
(B) 教材を本屋から買う
(C) 学生課で支払いをする
(D) コースの講師と話す

正解 A

よりぬき！テスト／解説／攻略法／トレーニング／確認テスト／解説／トレーニング

1つ目の文書（人事部長から Dewan さん宛の E メール）の❸に all fees will be covered by TVB Insurance「授業料は全て TVB Insurance が負担します」とあります。E メールの上部にあるメールアドレスから、TVB Insurance は Dewan さんが働く会社名だと分かるので、Dewan さんの授業料は会社が負担することが読み取れます。3つ目の文書（支払いに関するお知らせ）の❼では、This does not apply to those whose fees are being paid by their employer.「これは雇用主によって授業料を支払われている方々には適用されません」とあるので、文書前半に書かれている教科書代の支払い方法について Dewan さんは該当しないことが分かります。さらに❽で、In such cases, kindly collect an invoice from student affairs and give it to the relevant person in your workplace.「この場合、お手数ですが学生課から（教科書代の）請求書を受け取り、職場の担当者にお渡しください」とあります。invoice「請求書」を bill「請求書」、relevant person in your workplace「職場の担当者」を employer「雇用主」と言い換えて表している（A）が正解です。

❗本文→選択肢の言い換え

give it（=invoice）to the relevant person in your workplace
　　➡ Pass a bill to his employer

語句

□ need to do ～する必要がある　□ regarding ～について
□ course book 教科書　□ pass ～を渡す　□ bill 請求書
□ talk to ～に話し掛ける

25. In the notice, the phrase "apply to" in paragraph 1, line 6, is closest in meaning to

(A) request
(B) concern
(C) administer
(D) repair

お知らせの第１段落・６行目にある "apply to" に最も近い意味が近いのは

(A) ～を依頼する
(B) ～に関係する
(C) ～を運営する
(D) ～を直す

正解 B

解説

３つ目の文書（お知らせ）の❼に This does not apply to those whose fees are being paid by their employer. 「これは雇用主によって授業料が支払われている方々には適用されません」とあります。ここでの apply to は、does not apply to で「～には適用されない」という意味で使われています。これは does not concern「～には関係がない」とほぼ同じ意味になるため、正解は (B) です。

語句
☐ paragraph 段落　☐ be closest in meaning to ～に意味が最も近い

One-up apply の代表的な使い方

動詞の apply は自動詞で、後ろに続く前置詞によって意味が変わります。また、派生語も頻出のものばかりなので、ここでまとめて押さえておきましょう。

① apply for　～に申し込む
② apply to　～に適用する
③ application　申し込み、申込書
④ applicant　応募者

Chapter
4

トレーニング
確認テストで
スラッシュリーディングと音読

トレーニング
英文ストックを増やす

「確認テスト」で使用した問題文についても、スラッシュリーディングのトレーニング用テキストと音声を用意しました。

　Chapter2 で行ったのと同じように、使用されている語句や文法事項をしっかり確認し、スラッシュリーディングと音読に取り組んでください。

　スラッシュリーディングで英語の語順のまま理解できるようになったら、音読を繰り返し、ストックを増やしていきましょう。

スラッシュリーディング　トレーニング ①

Questions 1-2 / refer to / the following advertisement.
問題 1-2 は / ～に関するものです / 次の広告

Tekkin X:　Tekkin X：
The latest soccer boots　最新のサッカーシューズ
from the footwear specialist,　靴の専門家からの
Varhaven Outdoors.　Varhaven Outdoors

Tekkin X boots are the ultimate choice　Tekkin X は最高の選択です
for comfort and durability　快適さと耐久性のために
for the serious player.　真剣に取り組む選手にとって

Special coating keeps / feet dry　特別なコーティングが保ちます / 足をドライに
even in the wettest conditions　湿度の高い状態においても
Hand-stitched / in Germany　手縫いされました / ドイツで
by our craftspeople　私たちの職人によって
Available in electric yellow / and classic navy　蛍光イエローがあります / そしてクラシックネイビーも

As with all our boots,　当社の全ての靴と同様に
they come in / a range of sizes　それらは～の形で提供されます / 様々なサイズ

to fit / narrow and wide feet.　フィットするように / 幅が狭いそして広い足に
Get yours / today　あなたのものを手に入れてください / 今日
from your local sporting goods store　あなたの地元にあるスポーツ用品店から
- competitively priced at $95.00.　どこにも負けない低価格である 95 ドルで
You can find / further information / on Tekkin X,　見つけることができます / 詳しい情報を / Tekkin X についての
together with / our range of sneakers and ski boots,　〜と共に / 当社のスニーカーとスキー靴
by visiting www.varhavenoutdoors.org.　www.varhavenoutdoors.org. を訪れることによって

音読 トレーニング ①

Questions 1-2 refer to the following advertisement.　 Track 14

Tekkin X: The latest soccer boots from the footwear specialist, Varhaven Outdoors.

Tekkin X boots are the ultimate choice for comfort and durability for the serious player.

- Special coating keeps feet dry even in the wettest conditions
- Hand-stitched in Germany by our craftspeople
- Available in electric yellow and classic navy

As with all our boots, they come in a range of sizes to fit narrow and wide feet. Get yours today from your local sporting goods store - competitively priced at $95.00. You can find further information on Tekkin X, together with our range of sneakers and ski boots, by visiting www.varhavenoutdoors.org.

Questions 3-4 / refer to / the following notice.
問題 3-4 は / 〜に関するものです / 次のお知らせ

ATTENTION　注意

This access path　このアクセス経路
to the summit of Mt. Bencoe　Bencoe 山の頂上への
will be closed　閉鎖されます
from November to March.　11 月から 3 月まで
During that period,　その期間
please do not attempt / to open the gate　試みないでください / 門を開けることを
or continue on foot.　あるいは徒歩で進み続けることを
Sudden snow and rain storms / in winter　急な吹雪や暴風雨 / 冬の
can make / any ascent of Mt. Bencoe　する可能性がある / Bencoe 山へのいかなる登山を
extremely dangerous.　極端に危険に
Access is granted　アクセスは保証されます
only to road and forestry maintenance staff.　道と森の保守担当者だけに
If the gate is locked / outside the stated period,　門がロックされている場合は / 上記の期間外に
please call / Inverness Council's recreation division　電話してください / Inverness 地方議会のレクリエーション課
on 024-555-3859.　024-555-3859 に

音読 トレーニング ②

Questions 3-4 refer to the following notice. 🎧 Track 15

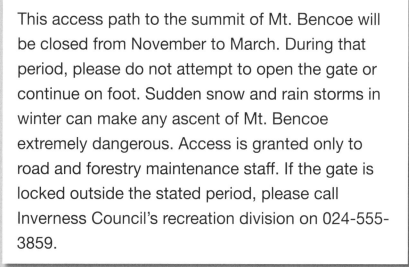

ATTENTION

This access path to the summit of Mt. Bencoe will be closed from November to March. During that period, please do not attempt to open the gate or continue on foot. Sudden snow and rain storms in winter can make any ascent of Mt. Bencoe extremely dangerous. Access is granted only to road and forestry maintenance staff. If the gate is locked outside the stated period, please call Inverness Council's recreation division on 024-555-3859.

Questions 5-7 / refer to / the following coupon.
問題 5-7 は / 〜に関するものです / 次のクーポン

Arusa Café　Arusa Café
Quality Coffee, / Great Times　質の高いコーヒー / 素晴らしい時間

To celebrate / the March reopening　〜を祝して / 3 月の再オープン
of our Fifth Street, Fakeham branch,　私たちの 5 番通り Fakeham の支店の
please use / this beverage coupon　お使いください / この飲み物クーポンを
anytime / until the end of May.　いつでも / 5 月末まで
The coupon can be used　クーポンを使うことができます
on any standard menu item,　どの通常メニュー商品に対しても
excluding fresh juices　フレッシュジュースを除いて
and frozen yogurts.　そしてフローズンヨーグルトも（除いて）

This coupon can only be used　このクーポンは〜だけ使えます
with orders exceeding $10.00.　10 ドルを超える注文に
There is a limit　制限があります
of one free beverage / per coupon.　1 杯の無料ドリンクという / クーポンごとに
Further copies can be made　追加のコピーが作れます
by visiting our Web site.　私たちのウェブサイトを訪れることによって
This promotion applies　このプロモーションは適用されます
only to the Fifth Street, Fakeham outlet / of Arusa Café.　5 番通り Fakeham
の店舗だけで / Arusa Café の
www.arusa-cafe.co.uk　www.arusa-cafe.co.uk

音読 トレーニング ③

Questions 5-7 refer to the following coupon.　　　🎧 Track 16

Arusa Café

Quality Coffee, Great Times

To celebrate the March reopening of our Fifth Street, Fakeham branch, please use this beverage coupon anytime until the end of May. The coupon can be used on any standard menu item, excluding fresh juices and frozen yogurts.

This coupon can only be used with orders exceeding $10.00. There is a limit of one free beverage per coupon. Further copies can be made by visiting our Web site. This promotion applies only to the Fifth Street, Fakeham outlet of Arusa Café.

www.arusa-cafe.co.uk

Questions 8-11 / refer to / the following article.
問題 8-11 は / 〜に関するものです / 次の記事

What's Happening / in Corkstone　何が起きている / Corkstone で

CORKSTONE (July 10)　CORKSTONE 7 月 10 日
— Residents going to Corkstone train station　Corkstone 駅に向かう住民たちは
may want to rethink / how they get there.　考え直した方がいいかもしれない /
どうやってそこに行くのかを
In line with the city's stated goal　市の述べていた目標に従って
of reducing carbon emissions / from local travel,　炭素排出削減の / 地元の交通
からの
a new building / for parking bicycles　新しい建物 / 自転車を駐車するための
has opened / beside the station.　オープンした / 駅のそばに

City officials hope　市の職員は願っている
the free-to-use facility / will encourage more citizens　無料で使える施設は / よ
り多くの市民を促す
to cycle to the station.　駅に自転車で行くことを
The building features / secure parking,　建物は特徴としている / 安全な駐輪場を
and the enclosed space / protects bicycles　そして囲まれた場所は / 自転車を
守る
from the weather.　天候から
The running costs will be partly funded　運営費用は一部資金提供される
by increased car parking charges　増加した駐車料金によって
around the station area.　駅のある地域の辺りの
It is hoped / that　期待される / 〜ということ
the fees will further push people　この料金がさらに人々を押す
to change their habits.　彼らの習慣を変えるように
Although there is no charge,　料金はかからないが
passes are needed / to use the bicycle parking.　許可証が必要とされる / 駐輪
場を使うためには

This allows City Hall / to monitor user numbers.　これは市役所ができるようにする / 利用者番号を管理することを

People can get one　人々はそれ（許可証）を手に入れられる

directly from the office / at the facility's entrance.　直接オフィスから / 施設の入り口で

Bicycle shop owner Liam Kane / welcomed the policy.
自転車店オーナーの Liam Kane は / その方針を歓迎した

"It's a fantastic way / to promote cycling.　これは素晴らしい方法です / サイクリングを奨励する

Bicycles are great　自転車は素晴らしいです

for the earth / and for your health."　地球にとって / そして各自の健康にとって

Mayor Harrison commented,　Harrison 市長はコメントした

"We're seeing / more and more families　私たちは見ることになる / ますます多くの家族たちを

choosing to live / in Corkstone,　住むことを選ぶ / Corkstone に

which is wonderful,　それは素晴らしい

but it must not lead / to increased traffic / on our roads.　しかしそれはつながってはいけない / 交通量の増加に / 私たちの道路で

Journeys made by bicycle / have a part to play　自転車での移動は / 一部の役割を担う

in keeping cars off the road."　車を道から減らすことにおいて

🎧 Track 17

What's Happening in Corkstone

CORKSTONE (July 10)— Residents going to Corkstone train station may want to rethink how they get there. In line with the city's stated goal of reducing carbon emissions from local travel, a new building for parking bicycles has opened beside the station.

City officials hope the free-to-use facility will encourage more citizens to cycle to the station. The building features secure parking, and the enclosed space protects bicycles from the weather. The running costs will be partly funded by increased car parking charges around the station area. It is hoped that the fees will further push people to change their habits. Although there is no charge, passes are needed to use the bicycle parking. This allows City Hall to monitor user numbers. People can get one directly from the office at the facility's entrance.

Bicycle shop owner Liam Kane welcomed the policy. "It's a fantastic way to promote cycling. Bicycles are great for the earth and for your health." Mayor Harrison commented, "We're seeing more and more families choosing to live in Corkstone, which is wonderful, but it must not lead to increased traffic on our roads. Journeys made by bicycle have a part to play in keeping cars off the road."

スラッシュリーディング トレーニング ⑤

Questions 12-15 / refer to / the following online chat discussion.
問題 12-15 は / ～に関するものです / 次のオンラインチャットの話し合い

Michelle Groves [10:20 A.M.]:　Michelle Groves 午前 10 時 20 分
Good morning / Anna and Pascal.　おはようございます / Anna と Pascal
Most of the details　詳細の大部分
of your catering order / have been finalized.　あなたのケータリングの注文 / 最終決定に入っています
I'll be making the necessary purchases / today and tomorrow.　私は必要なものを購入します / 今日と明日
I just need to confirm　私はちょっと確認する必要があります
whether there are any dietary needs or not.　何らかの食事に関するご要望があるかどうか

Anna Nakamura [10:22 A.M.]:　Anna Nakamura 午前 10 時 22 分
Hi Michelle.　こんにちは、Michelle
What do you mean / exactly?　どういうことですか / 正確には

Michelle Groves [10:23 A.M.]:　Michelle Groves 午前 10 時 23 分
For example,　例えば
some people may be allergic to nuts　ナッツにアレルギーがある人もいるかも
or perhaps / some do not eat meat.　またはおそらく / 肉を食べない人もいます

Anna Nakamura [10:25 A.M.]:　Anna Nakamura 午前 10 時 25 分
I get you.　分かりました
Pascal will know that　Pascal がそのことを知っていると思います
better than me.　私よりも
Pascal?　Pascal ?

Pascal Levant [10:28 A.M.]:　Pascal Levant 午前 10 時 28 分
No one has mentioned / anything to me.　誰も言ってきていません / 何も私に

Michelle Groves [10:30 A.M.]:　Michelle Groves 午前 10 時 30 分
OK.　分かりました
I'm planning / to top the cake with nuts,　私は予定しています / ケーキの上に
ナッツをのせる
so I'll go ahead with that.　それで進めますね
And there will some basic vegetarian dishes / anyway.　そして基本的なベジタ
リアン用の料理もあります / とにかく

Anna Nakamura [10:31 A.M.]:　Anna Nakamura 午前 10 時 31 分
Good to know.　教えてくれてありがとう
What time can we expect you　何時だと思っておけばいいですか
to arrive on the 23rd?　23 日に来ることについて

Michelle Groves [10:33 A.M.]:　Michelle Groves 午前 10 時 33 分
Around 11.　11 時くらいです
That reminds me　それで思い出しました
– will it be possible　可能でしょうか
to leave my van / near the main entrance?　私のバンを置いておくこと / メイン
エントランスのそばに
I have a lot of things to unload,　私はたくさん降ろすものがあります
and I'd rather not carry them / too far.　そしてそれらを運びたくはないのです /
あまり遠くまで

Anna Nakamura [10:36 A.M.]:　Anna Nakamura 午前 10 時 36 分
Leave it to me.　お任せください
I'll make sure　確実にやります
there's a space / for you.　スペースを確保します / あなたのために

Pascal Levant [10:38 A.M.]:　Pascal Levant 午前 10 時 38 分
And I'll be there / to greet you　そして私はそこにいます / あなたを出迎えるため
に
when you arrive.　あなたが着くときに
Everything needs to be perfect　全てのことは完璧でなくてはいけません
for our German colleagues.　私たちのドイツの同僚たちのために

We want them to experience / some genuine American hospitality!　私たちは
彼らに体験してほしいです / 本当のアメリカのおもてなしを

音読 トレーニング ⑤

Questions 12-15 refer to the following online chat discussion.　 Track 18

Michelle Groves [10:20 A.M.]: Good morning Anna and Pascal. Most of the details of your catering order have been finalized. I'll be making the necessary purchases today and tomorrow. I just need to confirm whether there are any dietary needs or not.

Anna Nakamura [10:22 A.M.]: Hi Michelle. What do you mean exactly?

Michelle Groves [10:23 A.M.]: For example, some people may be allergic to nuts or perhaps some do not eat meat.

Anna Nakamura [10:25 A.M.]: I get you. Pascal will know that better than me. Pascal?

Pascal Levant [10:28 A.M.]: No one has mentioned anything to me.

Michelle Groves [10:30 A.M.]: OK. I'm planning to top the cake with nuts, so I'll go ahead with that. And there will some basic vegetarian dishes anyway.

Anna Nakamura [10:31 A.M.]: Good to know. What time can we expect you to arrive on the 23rd?

Michelle Groves [10:33 A.M.]: Around 11. That reminds me – will it be possible to leave my van near the main entrance? I have a lot of things to unload, and I'd rather not carry them too far.

Anna Nakamura [10:36 A.M.]: Leave it to me. I'll make sure there's a space for you.

Pascal Levant [10:38 A.M.]: And I'll be there to greet you when you arrive. Everything needs to be perfect for our German colleagues. We want them to experience some genuine American hospitality!

Questions 16-20 / refer to / the following article and e-mail.
問題 16-20 は / 〜に関するものです / 次の記事と E メール

19 April ― 　4 月 19 日
Vue Garden Hotel Group will open / another hotel　Vue Garden Hotel Group
はオープンします / もう 1 つのホテルを
in Pattaya / later this year,　Pattaya に / 今年中に
which will bring / much-needed jobs / to the area.　それはもたらす / 待ち望ま
れていた仕事を / その地域に
The hotel will have 150 rooms　ホテルは 150 部屋を持つ予定だ
along with formal meeting facilities,　フォーマルな会議施設と共に
as Vue Garden hopes / to attract business travelers　Vue Garden は望んでい
るので / ビジネス旅行者を呼び込むこと
as well as traditional vacationers.　従来の行楽客と同様に
Unlike the group's existing hotel / in the town,　グループの既存のホテルとは
違って / 町にある
this one will feature / exclusive access / to a 100-meter stretch of beach　こ
のホテルは特徴とする / 独占的なアクセス / 100 メートルにわたるビーチへの
to enjoy swimming　泳ぎを楽しむための
in the bay's crystal clear waters.　入り江の透き通った水の中で
Plans also show / an upscale dining option,　計画はさらに示す / 高級な飲食店
の選択肢
a gym and sauna, / and an event hall.　ジムとサウナ / そしてイベントホール

People wishing to apply for a position / at the hotel,　求人に応募したいと考え
ている人は / ホテルの
which will open in October,　それは 10 月にオープンする
should visit / the group's Web site　訪れるべきだ / グループのウェブサイトを
and complete / the job application form.　そして記入する（べきだ）/ 仕事の応
募フォームに
According to a Vue Garden statement,　Vue Garden の声明によると
people with experience　経験のある人は

in customer service or room cleaning　顧客サービスや客室清掃の

are especially needed.　特に必要とされる

However, / the group is looking to hire young people　けれども / グループは若者を採用しようとしている

with no previous work experience　以前の仕事経験のない

as part of their kitchen crew　彼らのキッチンクルーの一部として

in order to train them　彼らを教育するために

in Vue Garden's unique cooking methods.　Vue Garden の独特な調理法において

The application deadline is July 1,　応募の締め切りは７月１日だ

with training for new employees　新しい従業員の研修が

beginning one month later.　１カ月後に始まる

音読 トレーニング ⑥

Questions 16-20 refer to the following article and e-mail.　🎧 Track 19

19 April — Vue Garden Hotel Group will open another hotel in Pattaya later this year, which will bring much-needed jobs to the area. The hotel will have 150 rooms along with formal meeting facilities, as Vue Garden hopes to attract business travelers as well as traditional vacationers. Unlike the group's existing hotel in the town, this one will feature exclusive access to a 100-meter stretch of beach to enjoy swimming in the bay's crystal clear waters. Plans also show an upscale dining option, a gym and sauna, and an event hall.

People wishing to apply for a position at the hotel, which will open in October, should visit the group's Web site and complete the job application form. According to a Vue Garden statement, people with experience in customer service or room cleaning are especially needed. However, the group is looking to hire young people with no previous work experience as part of their kitchen crew in order to train them in Vue Garden's unique cooking methods. The application deadline is July 1, with training for new employees beginning one month later.

To: Ally Thongsuk <happyally@usendmail.com>
宛先：Ally Thongsuk <happyally@usendmail.com>
From: Henri Poll <poll.h@vuegardenhotel.com>
送信者：Henri Poll <poll.h@vuegardenhotel.com>
Date: 5 June　日付：7月5日
Subject: Job application　件名：仕事への応募
Attachment: Information　添付：資料

Dear Ms. Thongsuk,　Thongsuk 様

Thank you for / completing an online application　～してくれてありがとうございます / オンライン応募に記入したこと
for our new hotel / in Pattaya.　私たちの新しいホテルの / Pattaya の
After careful consideration,　熟考した結果
we would like you to attend an interview　私たちはあなたに面接に参加していただきたい
to discuss your desire / to join us　あなたのご希望について話し合うために / 私たちに加わるという
as a junior kitchen assistant.　ジュニア・キッチンアシスタントとして
Interviews will be held　面接は行われます
at Quantum Business Park / on 14 July.　Quantum Business Park で / 7月14日に
Please see / the attached information　見てください / 添付の資料を
for directions and times.　道順と日時について
There is a frequent public bus service / to the park.　頻繁な公共バスの運行があります / 公園行きの

We expect all applicants / to arrive on time　私たちは全ての応募者に期待しています / 時間どおり到着することを
and to be formally dressed.　そして正装であることも
As the interview will take place / over two sessions,　面接は行われるので / 2つのセッションにわたって

234

a complimentary lunch will be provided. 無料の昼食が支給されます

As preparation for the interview, 面接への準備として

we hope 私たちは願います

you can research / Vue Garden's mission statement and history. あなたは調べることができる / Vue Garden の企業理念と歴史を

These can be found / on our Web site. これらは見つけられます / 私たちのウェブサイトで

Warmest regards, よろしくお願いいたします

Henri Poll   Henri Poll

Assistant Manager   アシスタントマネージャー

To:	Ally Thongsuk <happyally@usendmail.com>
From:	Henri Poll <poll.h@vuegardenhotel.com>
Date:	5 July
Subject:	Job application
Attachment:	Information

Dear Ms. Thongsuk,

Thank you for completing an online application for our new hotel in Pattaya. After careful consideration, we would like you to attend an interview to discuss your desire to join us as a junior kitchen assistant. Interviews will be held at Quantum Business Park on 14 July. Please see the attached information for directions and times. There is a frequent public bus service to the park.

We expect all applicants to arrive on time and to be formally dressed. As the interview will take place over two sessions, a complimentary lunch will be provided. As preparation for the interview, we hope you can research Vue Garden's mission statement and history. These can be found on our Web site.

Warmest regards,

Henri Poll
Assistant Manager

スラッシュリーディング　トレーニング ⑧

Questions 21-25 / refer to / the following e-mail, brochure, and notice.
問題 21-25 は / 〜に関するものです / 次の E メール、パンフレット、お知らせ

From: human.resources@tvb-insurance.com
送信者：human.resources@tvb-insurance.com
To: dewan.v@tvb-insurance.com
宛先：dewan.v@tvb-insurance.com
Date: 9 September　日付：9 月 9 日
Subject: Reach Out courses　件名：Reach Out コース

Dear Vikram Dewan,　Vikram Dewan 様

We at Human Resources received notification　私たち人事部は通知を受け取りました

through your section head, Paula Ingram,　あなたの部門長 Paula Ingram を通して

of your interest / in completing a course　あなたの関心について / コースを履修することの

at our training partner, Reach Out Education.　私たちの研修パートナーである Reach Out Education で

We will be delighted to support you　私たちは喜んであなたをサポートします

in your wish　あなたの願いを

to improve and update / your first aid skills.　向上させ最新のものにするという / あなたの応急処置技能を

This will benefit　これは恩恵を与えます

not only you, / but those around you　あなただけでなく / あなたの周りの人にも

if there is ever an accident　もし事故があった場合

or injury / in the office.　もしくは怪我が（あった場合）/ オフィスで

After finishing the course,　コースを修了した後

we may ask you　私たちはあなたにお願いをするかもしれません

to run an informal workshop　非公式のワークショップの開催を

for your colleagues　あなたの同僚たち向けに

to pass on your skills.　あなたのスキルを伝えるための

The course will be held　コースは行われます
at Reach Out's office / in central Leeds　Reach Out の事務所で / Leeds の中心
部にある
on every Tuesday / in October and November.　毎週火曜日に / 10 月と 11 月に
Needless to say,　言うまでも無く
you will be given / paid time off　あなたは与えられます / 有給休暇を
to attend the course,　そのコースに出席するために
and all fees will be covered　そして全ての料金が負担されます
by TVB Insurance.　TVB Insurance によって

I will forward you / further information　あなたに送ります / さらなる情報を
as I receive it / from Reach Out.　それを受け取り次第 / Reach Out から

Sally Milligan　Sally Milligan
Head of Human Resources　人事部長

音読 トレーニング ⑧

Questions 21-25 refer to the following e-mail, brochure, and notice.

🎧 Track 21

From:	human.resources@tvb-insurance.com
To:	dewan.v@tvb-insurance.com
Date:	9 September
Subject:	Reach Out courses

Dear Vikram Dewan,

We at Human Resources received notification through your section head, Paula Ingram, of your interest in completing a course at our training partner, Reach Out Education. We will be delighted to support you in your wish to improve and update your first aid skills. This will benefit not only you, but those around you if there is ever an accident or injury in the office. After finishing the course, we may ask you to run an informal workshop for your colleagues to pass on your skills.

The course will be held at Reach Out's office in central Leeds on every Tuesday in October and November. Needless to say, you will be given paid time off to attend the course, and all fees will be covered by TVB Insurance.

I will forward you further information as I receive it from Reach Out.

Sally Milligan
Head of Human Resources

Reach Out Education　Reach Out Education
32-35 Hanover St.　32-35 Hanover St.
Leeds LS2 9OL　Leeds LS2 9OL
Tel: (0133) 555-4040　電話 (0133) 555-4040

Reach Out Education's classroom-based courses　Reach Out Education の教室中心のコースは
cover a wide variety of topics　様々なトピックをカバーします
aimed at those / in work,　人たちを対象に / 働いている（人たち）
in education, / or searching for employment.　教育での（人たち）/ もしくは雇用を探している（人たち）
Passing one of our programs / means　私たちのプログラムの一つを修了することは / ～を意味します
you'll leave / with a nationally-recognized qualification　あなたは去るでしょう / 全国的に認められた資格と共に
to boost your career prospects.　あなたのキャリアの見込みを上向きにする
With maximum class sizes of fifteen people,　クラスの最大人数は 15 人で
each student has plenty of time　各生徒は十分な時間を持っています
with both their lead course instructor and assistant teacher.　コースの主任講師とアシスタント講師の両方と一緒の

October-November Class Offerings　10 月 -11 月の授業の内容
on Workplace Safety　職場の安全に関する

Hygiene　衛生学
For food preparation staff.　食品を調理するスタッフ向け
Learn the essentials　要点を学ぶ
of safe food handling techniques and cleanliness　安全に食品を扱う技術と清浄の
in order to prevent sickness　病気を避けるために
and to comply with national laws.　そして国の法律を遵守するために

Fire Safety　火災安全

This class covers / what to do　この授業は扱います / 何をすべきか

in a fire emergency.　火災緊急時において

Learn how to act,　どのように行動すべきかを学ぶ

how to direct colleagues to safety,　どのように同僚を安全へ導くか

and basic survival skills.　そして基本的な生存するための技術を

You'll also learn / fire prevention strategies.　あなたはさらに学ぶ / 火災予防戦略も

Working Smart　賢く働く

Study techniques / on avoiding / common workplace injuries

技術を学ぶ / 避けることについて / よくある職場での怪我を

that often happen　それはしばしば起こります

when lifting heavy items　重いものを持ち上げるときに

or not using the correct equipment.　もしくは正しい機材を使わなかったときに

This can lead / to a CityTec qualification　これはつながる可能性があります / CityTec の資格に

in workplace safety.　職場の安全において

Quick Response　迅速な反応

Learn / how to deal with / a variety of medical emergencies　学ぶ / どのように対処すべきか / 様々な医療的緊急事態に

before the professionals arrive.　専門家が到着する前に

Your quick actions could save / the life of a colleague.　あなたの迅速な行動が救えるかもしれません / 同僚の命を

The course covers / basic biology,　コースは〜を扱います / 基本的な生物学

covering wounds, / and treating shock.　傷を保護すること / そしてショック状態の手当ても

🎧 Track 22

Reach Out Education
32-35 Hanover St.
Leeds LS2 9OL
Tel: (0133) 555-4040

Reach Out Education's classroom-based courses cover a wide variety of topics aimed at those in work, in education, or searching for employment. Passing one of our programs means you'll leave with a nationally-recognized qualification to boost your career prospects. With maximum class sizes of fifteen people, each student has plenty of time with both their lead course instructor and assistant teacher.

October-November Class Offerings on Workplace Safety

Hygiene
For food preparation staff. Learn the essentials of safe food handling techniques and cleanliness in order to prevent sickness and to comply with national laws.

Fire Safety
This class covers what to do in a fire emergency. Learn how to act, how to direct colleagues to safety, and basic survival skills. You'll also learn fire prevention strategies.

Working Smart
Study techniques on avoiding common workplace injuries that often happen when lifting heavy items or not using the correct equipment. This can lead to a CityTec qualification in workplace safety.

Quick Response
Learn how to deal with a variety of medical emergencies before the professionals arrive. Your quick actions could save the life of a colleague. The course covers basic biology, covering wounds, and treating shock.

スラッシュリーディング　トレーニング ⑩

NOTICE　お知らせ

The policy on payments for textbooks　教科書の支払いに関する方針が
has changed.　変わりました
Course fees will no longer include / the cost of course materials.
コース料金はもはや含みません / 教材費を
Please pay for your textbooks　あなたの教科書の支払いをしてください
on the day of your first class　授業の初日に
by going to the student affairs office / on the first floor.　学生課に行くことに
よって / 1 階にある
Remember to bring / your student identification number.　忘れずに持参してく
ださい / あなたの学生証の番号を
This does not apply to those　これは人々には適用されません
whose fees are being paid　その人の料金が支払われている
by their employer.　雇用主によって
In such cases,　その場合は
kindly collect an invoice　お手数ですが請求書を受け取ってください
from student affairs　学生課から
and give it / to the relevant person　そしてそれを渡してください / 担当者に
in your workplace.　あなたの職場の
Students repeating courses / should check with their lead instructor　コース
再履修の学生は / 主任講師に相談してください
to confirm / that the course materials are unchanged.　確認する / 教材が変更
されていないことを

NOTICE

The policy on payments for textbooks has changed. Course fees will no longer include the cost of course materials. Please pay for your textbooks on the day of your first class by going to the student affairs office on the first floor. Remember to bring your student identification number. This does not apply to those whose fees are being paid by their employer. In such cases, kindly collect an invoice from student affairs and give it to the relevant person in your workplace. Students repeating courses should check with their lead instructor to confirm that the course materials are unchanged.

マークシート

Chapter 1, 3

Part 7 (学習日：　　月　　日／所要時間：　　分　　秒)

No.	ANSWER	🕐	No.	ANSWER	🕐	No.	ANSWER	🕐
1	Ⓐ Ⓑ Ⓒ Ⓓ	☐	11	Ⓐ Ⓑ Ⓒ Ⓓ	☐	21	Ⓐ Ⓑ Ⓒ Ⓓ	☐
2	Ⓐ Ⓑ Ⓒ Ⓓ	☐	12	Ⓐ Ⓑ Ⓒ Ⓓ	☐	22	Ⓐ Ⓑ Ⓒ Ⓓ	☐
3	Ⓐ Ⓑ Ⓒ Ⓓ	☐	13	Ⓐ Ⓑ Ⓒ Ⓓ	☐	23	Ⓐ Ⓑ Ⓒ Ⓓ	☐
4	Ⓐ Ⓑ Ⓒ Ⓓ	☐	14	Ⓐ Ⓑ Ⓒ Ⓓ	☐	24	Ⓐ Ⓑ Ⓒ Ⓓ	☐
5	Ⓐ Ⓑ Ⓒ Ⓓ	☐	15	Ⓐ Ⓑ Ⓒ Ⓓ	☐	25	Ⓐ Ⓑ Ⓒ Ⓓ	☐
6	Ⓐ Ⓑ Ⓒ Ⓓ	☐	16	Ⓐ Ⓑ Ⓒ Ⓓ	☐			
7	Ⓐ Ⓑ Ⓒ Ⓓ	☐	17	Ⓐ Ⓑ Ⓒ Ⓓ	☐			
8	Ⓐ Ⓑ Ⓒ Ⓓ	☐	18	Ⓐ Ⓑ Ⓒ Ⓓ	☐			
9	Ⓐ Ⓑ Ⓒ Ⓓ	☐	19	Ⓐ Ⓑ Ⓒ Ⓓ	☐			
10	Ⓐ Ⓑ Ⓒ Ⓓ	☐	20	Ⓐ Ⓑ Ⓒ Ⓓ	☐			

著者略歴

濵﨑潤之輔 （はまさき・じゅんのすけ）

大学・企業研修講師、書籍編集者。早稲田大学政治経済学部経済学科卒業。
TOEIC® L&Rテスト990点(満点)を70回以上取得。
現在は、明海大学、獨協大学、早稲田大学エクステンションセンターなど、全国の大学で講師を務めるかたわら、ファーストリテイリングや楽天銀行、SCSK(住友商事グループ)、エーザイ、オタフクソースといった大手企業でもTOEIC® L&Rテスト対策の研修講師を努める。
主催するTOEIC® L&Rテスト対策セミナーはいつも満席になるほどの人気で、スコアアップだけでなく英語力も身につけたい多くの人たちに支持されている。
著書に、「TOEIC® L&Rテスト990点攻略 改訂版」、「TOEIC® L&Rテスト 目標スコア奪取の模試」（旺文社）、「聞くだけでTOEIC® TESTのスコアが上がるCDブック」（アスコム）、「はじめて受けるTOEIC®テスト パーフェクト入門」（桐原書店）、「TOEIC® L&Rテスト壁越えトレーニング」シリーズ（旺文社）などがあり、監修した書籍も含めると累計60万部以上の実績を誇る。

ブログ：独学でTOEIC990点を目指す！：http://independentstudy.blog118.fc2.com/
Twitterアカウント：@HUMMER_TOEIC
Instagramアカウント：junnosuke_hamasaki

よりぬき！
TOEIC® L&Rテスト
飛躍のナビゲーター　Part 7

2020 年 9 月 26 日　初版　第 1 刷発行

著者	濵﨑潤之輔
発行者	天谷修平
発行	株式会社オープンゲート
	〒 101-0051
	東京都千代田区神田神保町 2-14 SP 神保町ビル 5 階
	TEL：03-5213-4125　FAX：03-5213-4126
印刷・製本	株式会社光邦

ISBN978-4-910265-05-6
©2020 Junnosuke Hamasaki

装丁	株式会社鷗来堂（川口美紀）
本文デザイン・DTP	株式会社鷗来堂
問題作成	株式会社 CPI Japan
編集協力	渡邉真理子
音声制作協力	株式会社ジェイルハウス・ミュージック
録音スタジオ	株式会社巧芸創作
ナレーション	Howard Colefield
	Karen Haedrich